Racquetball:
the Sport for Everyone

• How to Play • All the New Shots
• Offensive and Defensive Strategy • Doubles Play

By Randy Stafford

Published by Stafford Publishing Co.
2876 Putting Green
Memphis, TN 38115

Manufactured in the United States of America.
ISBN 0-9612954-0-6.

ABOUT THE AUTHOR...

Randy Stafford started playing racquetball in 1969 when he was 14 years old. While attending the University of Tennessee-Knoxville, he won the National Intercollegiate Singles title in 1974 and the National Intercollegiate Doubles in 1975. Randy turned professional at 20 years old and placed in the top eight in the first IRA "pro" tournament. He has participated in many national invitational singles and doubles tournaments over the years.

Currently, Randy continues to play regularly. He is a member of the teaching organization, American Professional Racquetball Organization, (APRO), gives clinics across the country, and has taught students of all ages and abilities. He also is president of The Court Company, one of the largest racquetball court construction companies in the country.

This third edition of *Racquetball: The Sport for Everyone* is a complete and updated revision of the original book Randy wrote and published in 1975.

Why does racquetball enjoy the popularity it does today? This question does not have one clear-cut answer, but many. Racquetball is no longer a fad; it fits right in with millions of peoples' lifestyles.

Have you noticed the fitness boom going on all around us today? Nearly everyone is attempting to jump on the bandwagon and participate in some form of fitness. In today's busy world, time is the most important commodity we have. And any type of fitness takes time. If you consider time spent exercising, racquetball is one of the best ways to concentrate the greatest amount of exercise into the shortest amount of time.

In a study by Dr. David Montgomery of McGill University made in 1983, heart rates as experienced by racquetball players were recorded. In comparisons of A, B and C level players who were matched in ability with opponents below and above them, the heart rate average was at least 70% of the predicted maximum heart rate. The average heart rate for equally matched players was 87% of the predicted maximum heart rate. Simply stated, racquetball appears to be an excellent aerobic sport.

Playing racquetball requires very little equipment. Basically, a pair of shorts, a shirt, tennis shoes, an inexpensive racquet, a can of balls, and eyeguards are all that is needed. Take fifteen minutes of instruction and you can actually finish the hour off with three exciting games of racquetball.

Racquetball is here to stay. Courts are built at every level of our society—from private clubs and churches to colleges, hotels and military bases. But why do people really play racquetball? Well, okay, forget the amount of exercise it offers. Forget the ease of play and temperature controlled climate. Forget the availability of courts. But after you play, you will never forget that *racquetball is just plain fun.*

In this book, I hope I will be able to stimulate the interest of any readers who are unfamiliar with the game and get them on a court. For those who are already playing the game, I hope to heighten their interest and aid them in improving their skills in the game.

For the beginner, I have described the fundamentals using concepts that will make them easier to learn. The intermediate player will find a detailed section on the various serves and shots, as well as tips on when and where to put them to use.

I have covered all aspects of racquetball; from grips to footwork, from concentration to diving and hinders. A significant amount of the text is devoted to strategy, including step-by-step instructions on how to play a tournament match, from the week before the tournament to the conclusion of the match.

Also included is a chapter on the unwritten rules of the game which will give the reader an insight into the ways players relate to each other and the treatment to which they are accustomed on and off the court.

Incorporated within this book is a new technique called "action ball." Simply described, "action ball" is a method of showing the various shots and angles of a ball in play so that it is easy for the reader to visualize the path of the ball. As you will notice, the normal illustrations and charts are replaced with photos using the "action ball" sequence.

As with any undertaking of this nature, there are many people who have helped in one way or another. I would like to sincerely thank them all for the tremendous work which has gone into this book.

For we are his workmanship, created in Christ Jesus for good works, which God prepared beforehand, that we should walk in them.

Ephesians 2:10

Randy Stafford

table of contents

Illustration 1-1 *Randy Stafford, left, and Larry Liles give Gloria Vaught some instructions.*

chapter 1

BEGINNING THE GAME

Although his name does not ring a loud bell like some of his fellow founding fathers, Joe Sobek assured himself of a place alongside the likes of Abner Doubleday and Dr. James Naismith when, in 1950, he became determined to find a game better than paddleball to play in a handball court.

Sobek was a squash pro when he began toying with the idea of using a racquet instead of a paddle. He took his idea to a manufacturer of racquets and eventually designed a racquet to his liking. His first order consisted of 25 racquets.

The first ball used in racquetball was a red and blue ball, the kind found then in the neighborhood five and ten. After he had used several of those, Sobek went to a ball manufacturer to find a ball suitable for his new game.

Sobek made some rules to go with his new racquet and ball, and sent the infant game of racquetball on its way.

The sport grew slowly until the late 1960's when it began to benefit from the leadership of Dr. Bud Muehleisen, who later became known as one of the founding fathers of racquetball. "Dr. Bud" promoted the game by giving clinics across the country and spawning interest in racquetball wherever he went. It was as much through his efforts as anyone's that the game enjoyed its biggest boom in the 1970's.

The International Racquetball Association (IRA) was established in 1968 to organize and improve the game. With its help, all kinds of tournaments—local, state, regional, national, and international—were started. The tournaments provided competition for players in all age groups and skill levels. Finally, in 1974, the IRA held its first professional tournament.

From a sport recently in its infancy, racquetball has now matured to a universally popular sport. All ages can enjoy and become proficient at the game. Racquetball is also becoming increasingly popular as a spectator sport. More and more courts are built with glass backwalls for spectator viewing, and the first four-wall glass court has just been completed in Atlanta. Tournaments draw ever larger crowds and top players are achieving national recognition outside the sport!

Today, the IRA is *The Amateur Racquetball Association* (AARA) which is the only official governing organization of amateur racquetball. Located in the Olympic Village of Colorado Springs, the AARA has a monthly newspaper devoted to the amateur player. Information on membership is available at the beginning of the rules chapter.

EQUIPMENT

Now that racquetball has matured as a sport, there is a wide range of equipment available for all players. For women, it is appropriate to wear shorts and a pullover shirt, a skirt or a tennis dress. Men usually wear shorts and a tee shirt. Both should try to wear cotton shirts which help keep you cooler than acrylic materials. Clothing should be loose fitting and you should avoid wearing dark clothing which occasionally will blend with the ball making it difficult to see.

• Shoes

There is some basic information you need before buying racquetball shoes. First of all, a pair of aerobic or jogging shoes should not be used for racquetball. This is because the soles of these shoes are not flexible and will have a tendency to roll over on the edge and sprain your ankle more easily than a flexible, rounded edge.

A good racquetball shoe will have a rounded edge along the sole as well as a flexible sole. I prefer the leather shoes over canvas as they offer a more comfortable fit and seem to last longer. However, canvas shoes are less expensive and may keep your feet cooler during extended play. High top shoes are frequently used for additional ankle support. Also, I recommend two pairs of socks to avoid blisters as well as cushion your feet during play.

• Racquets

There is also a wide choice of racquets on the market today, including aluminum, fiberglass and graphite. Generally, racquets weigh between 230 grams and 280 grams. Grips are sized between 3-5/16″ and 4-1/2″. Usually, women should use the smaller sizes and most men should use between 4″ and 4-1/2″ grips. I have a large hand, and while in tennis I use a 4-3/4″ grip, in racquetball I use a 4-1/8″ grip. The smaller grip size enables you to use more wrist action which is necessary in racquetball and described in later chapters. (An easy check is to grasp the grip and see if your middle and fourth fingers touch the skin at the base of your thumb.)

Another consideration is the size of the racquet. Mid-sized and oversized racquets are becoming increasingly popular and should be included in your racquet choices.

These racquets offer a larger sweet spot with a longer reach, and have been accepted for almost all tournament play. However, since these racquets are larger, in fast front court action you may find them a little slower to setup for quick shots than with conventional sized racquets. Practicing with the larger racquets (perhaps borrowed from a friend) will help you make your decision.

Strings should always consist of nylon. Tension on the strings should be between 20 and 28 pounds, depending on your racquet and game style. Gut strings are not used because they add no advantage at such low-stringing tension. According to the rules, and general safety, your thong (or wrist strap) should be worn on the wrist at all times so that if you lose your grip on the racquet, it will not fly across the court and strike your opponent. Remember, never play with anyone who does not have the thong secured around their wrist. The loop on the base of the racquet is slipped over the hand and the racquet twisted three or four times to secure the loop around the wrist during play. Another way to use the wrist strap that I feel is easier than the conventional twisted loopstyle is to untie the loop and then tie it off at the end secured to the racquet, making a long cord attached to the butt. Put one knot in the other end of the cord. Then, take that end and tie it around the cord coming from the racquet butt to form a loop. This loop will slide around your hand and then tighten on your wrist. I have found this slip loop to be much more comfortable than the conventional loop used on most racquets.

Purchasing your first racquet is an important step. There are a few ground rules you need to consider about your own style of game before you make a decision. Do you have a fast, hard stroke; a slower controlled stroke; or possibly a tennis stroke? Generally speaking, if you use a lot of wrist action with a fast stroke, a lighter racquet will suit your needs. However, if you have a slower controlled stroke, (like mine), a slightly heavier racquet is fine. Since all racquets are relatively light, there is no reason that a female should buy a light racquet and a man a heavier racquet. It all depends on your game style and type of stroke. If you do not know what type of game style you have, read on and borrow a racquet during the interim.

Another consideration in your racquet choice is its flexibility. Try to remember that usually the aluminum or metal racquets are stiff, while the composite racquets are more flexible, although this is not always be the case. Most hardhitters buy a stiff racquet to add to their power. I like to see the opposite happen so they can add some control to their power game.

Remember, stringing your racquet at different tensions can also make your racquet seem stiff or flexible. I would always recommend a flexible racquet because it is easier to control the ball and it absorbs some of

Illustration 1-2 *An approved ball from the AARA*

the shock from the impact of the ball during the stroke.

String inserts are a new phenomenom appearing on the racquetball horizon. These

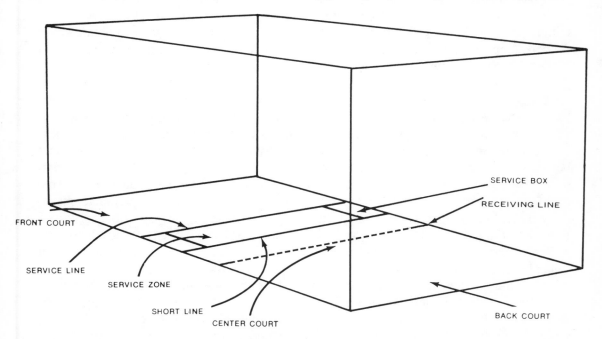

Illustration 1-3

Racquetball Court

are small rubber devices that are inserted between the strings to supposedly absorb the shock of the ball. In my opinion, the jury is still out on the amount of shock absorbed, but at the low price, it may well be worth your money to try them out for yourself.

• Balls

For years, I have been the official racquetball tester for the AARA. We tested all new balls submitted for approval by the respective companies, which in turn were placed on the market for sale if approved. There are some good and bad balls on the market today, but if the can is marked "AARA approved" these balls should be acceptable. I would recommend the pressureless balls, as they will last longer.

• Gloves

Gloves are a good idea if you have a problem with your racquet turning while hitting the ball. Also, it is nice to wear a glove if you wish to keep your hand soft and free from blisters. The disadvantage with a glove is that you lose some feel of the racquet. A good compromise are the fingerless gloves or the rubberized grips which are slipped over the leather handle. You can help keep a leather grip clean by placing a sock over the handle after you finish your game. Also, washing your hands to remove any oils will help considerably. Once your leather grip becomes dirty and worn, try washing it in hot, soapy water but be sure to allow plenty of time for it to dry before your next match. For glove users, I know a great way to keep the fingers of the glove stretched out straight while they dry after playing. Obtain a wooden spike about 8″ long and 1/2″ in diameter with rounded ends. After play, simply stick the spike down the fingerholes and stretch each finger back out. For convenience, carry the spike in your bag and it will help your glove

dry faster and in the proper position.

• Eyeguards

Last but not least, the eyeguards are one of the player's most important pieces of equipment. Eyeguards should be required for all players, whatever the age. This is the only common injury that could happen to anyone at any time on the court. There is no compromise to wearing eyeguards. You can learn to see equally as well while playing, as many pros do, because if you ever have an eye injury, it quite often can be permanent. Generally, racquetball is an injury-free sport, if and only if, you wear eyeguards. Many colleges are requiring all students to wear eyeguards (which is a super time to start players in the proper habit).

With over 70,000 eye injuries a year in racquetball alone, there is a growing emphasis to require eyeguards during all tournament play. However, it is essential that players wear quality eyeguards whenever they are on the court. How would you like to be hit in the eye with a ball traveling at 140 miles per hour? So keep those eyeguards on at all times.

Standards for acceptable eyeguards have been developed by various optical agencies, although none have been officially endorsed by the AARA. (However, eyeguards are required for any sanctioned AARA event if the participant is under 19.) As new and better eyeguards are appearing on the market, each player should research what is available and pick out the type that is best for their particular needs. Some glasses on the market are next to useless and can even be dangerous, so be sure to find quality, well made glasses. Many glasses with open eye slits do not prevent the ball from puncturing the eye when hit hard with a ball and are not recommended for use under any conditions. (Dr. Paul F. Vinger, Chairman of the ASTM Eye Safety Committee; National Racquetball Magazine, "Mandatory Eyeguards", February, 1986.) A few glasses have anti-fog treatments, but if you perspire heavily, try using a headband as well.

Two pair of eyeguards should be kept with the player's equipment in case one is damaged during play. Be sure to protect the glasses by keeping them in their protective coverings. They represent quite an investment. Any time eyeguards have been hit, they should be replaced immediately, even if damage to the eyeguards is not visible to the eye.

• Courts

This book is concerned primarily with four-wall racquetball, although the game also can be played on a three-wall or one-wall court. The four-wall court is 40 feet long, 20 feet wide and 20 feet high. The back wall, however, can be anywhere from 12 to 20 feet high.

The walls of the court are frequently panels made of plastic-laminated particleboard, similar to kitchen table tops. Some courts are plaster whereas others are simply painted concrete.

THE GAME

The game can be played with two people (singles), three people (cutthroat), or four people (doubles). In cutthroat, each player keeps his own score. Players earn points by scoring against their opponents. The server continues until he loses a point, after which a different player serves. The first player to accumulate 15 points wins. Doubles rules will be detailed in the Doubles chapter.

The basic rules of the game are as follows (additional information on rules can be found in Chapter Six and a complete listing of the rules can be found at the end of the book): Standing in the service zone, the server drops and hits the ball after the first bounce so that it hits the front wall on the fly. After hitting the front wall, the ball can hit a side wall, but must bounce on the floor before hitting a third wall. In addition, while serving, the ball cannot hit the back wall before it hits the floor. The ball cannot hit the ceiling at all during the serve. If the serve does not hit the front wall first, it is an automatic sideout (serve goes to the opponent).

If the ball does not land on the floor past the short line, or in the case of a three-wall serve or a serve that hits the back wall on the fly, the server is given one more opportunity to make a good serve.

Once the ball is correctly put into play, the player receiving the ball must hit it before it bounces twice, although he is allowed to hit it on the fly (before it hits the floor). After the ball is hit, it must make contact with the front wall before hitting the floor. The ball can hit any combination of ceiling, backwalls and side walls before hitting the front wall, as long as the ball does not touch the floor.

A sideout is called when the server loses a point. His opponent, or the opposing team, then gains the serve. Only the serving player or team can score. The first player or team that scores 15 points is the winner, even if the opposition has 14 points. In games and tournaments, the player who wins two out of three games wins the match. Tie breakers are to 11 points.

The rules of racquetball are always subject to change, so players are advised to continue checking for revisions.

(Note: The current AARA rules require the receiving line to extend in a dotted line all the way across the court. This has not been done in the succeeding diagrams in order to keep them simple.)

Stretching before a game will help prevent injuries.

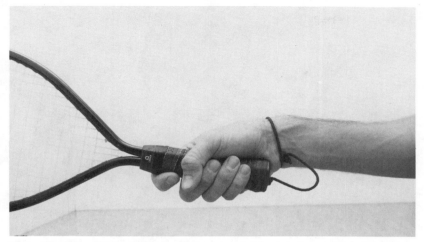

Illustration 2-1 *Notice the index finger extended for better control and the thong secured on the wrist for safety.*

chapter 2

FOREHAND, BACKHAND GRIPS AND STROKES

Learning to hold the racquet is like learning to drive a car. If you do not do it properly, you will suffer the consequences. Accidents will happen, because a slight error in gripping the racquet will result in a large error in the accuracy of your shot. If a player loses a match, probably the last cause he will consider is an improper grip when, possibly, it should have been the first.

The sooner a player becomes familiar with the grip, the better off he will be. It is difficult to hit a kill shot or a ceiling ball if you are thinking about how to hold the racquet. Learn the grip quickly and it will soon become second nature.

FOREHAND GRIP

For the basic forehand grip, take the throat of your racquet and hold it with your left hand. (Left-handers use the opposite hand.) Hold the racquet horizontally so that the strings are perpendicular to the floor. Put the palm of your right hand against the strings, keeping the hand flat against the racquet. Slide the open palm down until it is pressed against the grip (the hand should still be open). Without moving your palm, hold the grip so that your thumb and forefinger form a V at the top of the grip. (Illus. 2-2, 3, 4, 5).

With practice, you should automatically grip the racquet in this fashion. The fingers should be spaced slightly apart, with the forefinger extended up a bit for better control of slippage and for better accuracy. The racquet should eventually feel like a continuation of your hand.

For added control and prevention of slippage, keep your entire palm on the grip; do not allow it to slide over the end.

Illustration 2-2   Illustration 2-3

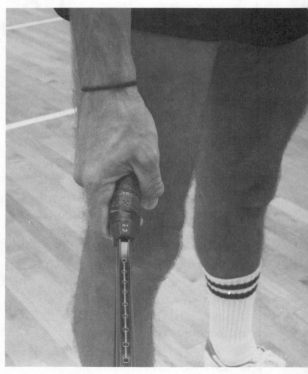

Illustration 2-4
These pictures illustrate the forehand grip. Place your hand on the strings as shown. Move your hand down the throat of the racquet and grasp the grip without turning the rac-

Illustration 2-5
quet. If done properly, this causes the V in your hand to be centered directly on top of the grip.

16

BACKHAND GRIP

The backhand grip is somewhat more complicated in that a slight adjustment from the forehand grip is necessary. There is no predetermined grip for each player. Some will make larger adjustments than others, and there are a few who will make no adjustment at all.

The necessity for the adjustment can be demonstrated by taking the racquet in a forehand grip and going through the motions of hitting a backhand. At the imaginary point of contact with the ball, the racquet will be angled slightly upward. Because the objective should be to hit the ball flat rather than with a slice, the adjustment should be made by rotating your hand counterclockwise around the grip, usually about one quarter of an inch. Left-handed

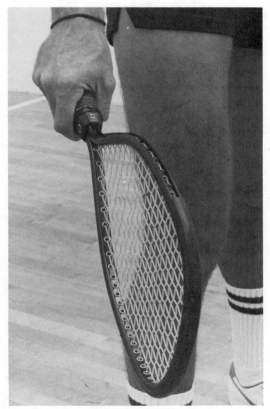

Illustration 2-6 *For the backhand grip, simply rotate your hand counterclockwise 1/4 inch from the proper forehand grip. Again, be sure the throng is secured on the wrist.*

players should rotate the hand clockwise. The adjustment should amount to whatever it takes to eliminate the slice and align the racquet perpendicular to the floor. (Illus. 2-6).

Like most other fundamentals in racquetball, the adjustment in grips will become habit after a certain amount of practice. It will become so automatic that, with the exception of a fast front court volley, the adjustment will be effected with ease and with time to spare. The lack of reaction time between front court volleys is such that there may not be time to change grips. In that case, it is advisable to adjust your arm instead of your grip. Simply rotate your arm a couple of degrees forward for a flat stroke.

Some advanced players will use the same grip for both the forehand and the backhand, but it is my belief that the slight shift for the backhand achieves more consistency and control. In summary, change grips whenever possible for better accuracy, or if there is not time for a grip change, adjust the arm instead. There will be ample time to change grips in all but a few instances.

Some people suggest using a different grip for certain shots (i.e., ceiling ball), but I definitely recommend developing the two grips as described above for all your shots in racquetball. An important key to remember in racquetball is that the action is so fast, you should always try to keep your fundamentals as simple as possible. Making the sport complicated will only cost you points in the long run.

STROKES

Before a player begins to practice strokes on a court, it is important that they warm-up their muscles. Several minutes of stretching and flexing exercises before and after play will help prevent injuries. A player should warm-up their muscles starting from the top of the body and move downward

Illustration 2-7   Illustration 2-8

Illustration 2-9

Illustration 2-10

Gloria demonstrates an easy method to obtain the correct forehand ready position. She holds her arm straight out with the proper grip. Next she cocks her wrist, then bends her elbow as shown. She then tucks her racquet behind her head, shifts her weight to her right side, bends her knees and leans over to form the ready position.

to the larger muscles of the torso and legs. Be sure to loosen up the neck and shoulder muscles as they are usually pretty stiff. Don't forget to warm-up immediately before play and cool down immediately afterwards. This cool down will help prevent muscle soreness the next day.

Now, back to the stroke. Anyone who has played tennis, golf, or baseball is well aware of the importance of the swing. The racquetball swing is a delicate, fluid motion that should be void of jerks, hooks, or other interruptions in its flow—the smoother, the better.

FOREHAND STROKE

The fastest way to learn the proper forehand stroke is to follow these easy steps. Follow the pictures carefully to see the details in the stroke. First, bending the legs slightly, hold your arms out from your body and start swinging your arms, rotating your body back and forth (Illus. 2-11, 12). This causes you to turn your upper body, hips and knees similar to a stroke in full motion. While doing this motion backward and forward, be sure to swing as far each way as you can. Now, with that motion in your mind, let us work on the rest of the stroke. Cock your wrist to the right if you are righthanded. Now bend your elbow so the racquet is sticking straight up in the air. Rotate your elbow away from your body and the racquet will end up right behind your head. If it is of any help, bend your elbow more toward your head in order to give you a tighter starting position. If you will bend your knees, shift your weight to the back foot and twist your body to the right—you are then in the ready position. (Illus. 2-7, 8, 9, 10). Remember the swinging session a few sentences back? The key now is to start using that motion as you begin turning your body into the shot, while

Illustration 2-11   Illustration 2-12

By swinging her body around, Gloria demonstrates the rotation of the upper body, hips and knees.

Illustration 2-13   Illustration 2-14

Illustration 2-15   Illustration 2-16
Randy demonstrates the proper form for the forehand stroke.

Illustration 2-17 *Proper forehand*   Illustration 2-18   Proper backhand

Illustration 2-19
Improper forehand form because arm is straight before contact with the ball.

Illustration 2-20
Improper backhand because elbow is too close to body during stroke.

keeping your knees bent. Start to rotate your shoulders and bring your arm around with your elbow leading your hand. As your body rotates gradually, unravel your arm as you extend your elbow. Your elbow should be away from your body at a comfortable distance. Only at contact with the ball will your arm be straight. At contact, right out from the front foot, you should snap your wrist. After contact, continue twisting your body, shifting your weight forward and following-through with the racquet across your body. Be sure not to restrict your follow-through. Your opposite hand should flow with your shoulders at about hip level. Try to be fluid. Rotate your shoulders and hips and let your body bring your arm around (Illus. 2-13, 14, 15, 16). Remember to gradually extend your arm as you start to swing. Many people extend their arm too soon which causes a loss of power.

BACKHAND STROKE

What is the best way to develop the backhand motion? Everybody has thrown a frisbee at one time or another. If you do not have one handy, let us just pretend. Try curling your arm and cocking your wrist while turning your body like you are ready to throw the frisbee. Go through the motion, being sure to rotate your hips and shoulders as you shift your weight forward. As you uncurl your arm at the point of release, simply fling your wrist. Let your upper body turn comfortably. This will give you your follow-through. It is that simple. (Illus. 2-22, 23, 24, 25).

If you are a beginner, absolutely do not use a ball when first trying to learn the forehand or backhand stroke. Practice the motion until it feels comfortable; then work on your wrist snap. At the point of contact (directly in front of your forward foot) your wrist snap should produce a quick, crisp swish. If you notice that the swish occurs during your follow-through, (which is typical), time your wrist action earlier and make it a very short sounding swish. Only after you feel comfortable with these strokes should you try using a ball. Hit a few shots, then practice swinging a few times without a ball. Turn those hips and shift that weight and you will develop a picture-perfect stroke before you know it.

Once you begin to play, there are several important safety guide lines that you should keep in mind at all times. Makes these a part of your game!

SAFETY TIPS

- Be sure you and your opponent are wearing eyeguards.
- Watch your opponent setup for the ball, then turn your face back to the direction you anticipate the ball will be hit. Never watch your opponent hit the ball.
- Know where your opponent is at all times.
- Don't crowd your opponent while they are shooting—give them room! Call a safety hinder if you feel your racquet or ball may possibly strike your opponent.
- Keep your thong attached to your wrist at all times, even during your warm-up strokes, and never play with someone whose thong is not secured.
- Play doubles only after you have become proficient at singles.

Illustration 2-22   Illustration 2-23

Illustration 2-24   Illustration 2-25

The effective backhand stroke begins with the proper ready position, continues with a smooth stroke, and ends with a good follow-through.

Illustration 3-1

Illustration 3-2

Illustration 3-3   *Randy demonstrates the high lob serve in these three photographs.*

chapter 3

SERVICE

Regardless of how skillful a player becomes in the many facets of racquetball, the weapons at his disposal can be rendered useless by a careless or ineffective serve. The serve initiates the action in each point during a match, and it could very well be a player's only shot of the point. His serve could be so strategically placed that his opponent is unable to make a return, or his serve could be so poorly executed that his opponent is able to hit a return for a winner.

Some players will choose to take the calculated risk of attempting difficult serves which, if properly executed, will likely earn them the point. If improperly executed, they likely will cause a player to lose the point. Obviously, a player must have considerable confidence in his serving ability to adopt this strategy.

Other players will choose to use the serve merely to begin a rally. It will be used as a weapon only to the point of gaining them a desirable position as the action begins.

The top players in racquetball today have changed the serve so that it can now make the difference between winning and losing. They have developed, as you can, a powerful and accurate serve. In today's racquetball, aces are very common. The serve is no longer simply a method of starting play, but a lethal weapon in the hands of the server that, if used properly, could be the reason for their winning. Remember that when serving, you have full control. It is the only time you can drop the ball and choose your shot before hitting it to your opponent. Take advantage of this and make your opponent move to his weak side giving the lowest percentage return and allowing you time to set up for the service return.

SERVES

There are several serves available for each plan of attack. There is a lob serve and a garbage serve (low lob serve), high and low "Z" serves, and drive serves. Try serving most of your serves from the middle of the service zone. From this area you have more shots available, thus making your opponent guess what you are hitting. For the Z serve you may have to take a couple of steps to one side of the center to obtain the proper angle. All of these serves have their distinct advantages as well as pitfalls.

• Lob Serve

The advantage of a lob serve is that it forces your opponent to make his return from deep in the court (the last fifth, if the court were divided into five sectors). It also affords you, the server, plenty of time to get into position for your next shot. If your opponent is playing at a rapid pace, the lob serve will slow him down a bit.

In hitting the lob serve, the object, as implied above, is to make the ball land deep in the court. Caution must be taken not to hit the ball so hard that it bounces off the back wall for an easy return. Ideally, the serve will come off the front wall in a high arc and hit the side wall in the last fifth of the court, bounce low and softly away from the wall and die before hitting the back wall. (Illus. 3-4).

The server should position himself in the center of the service area, allowing him to

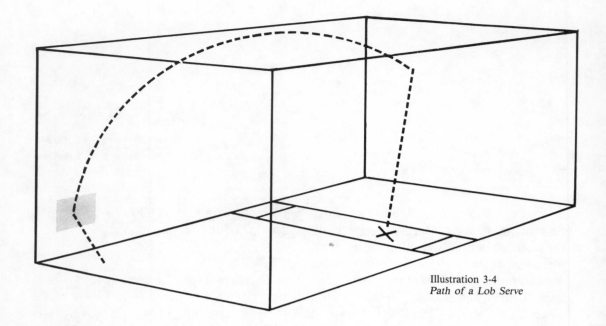

Illustration 3-4
Path of a Lob Serve

hit toward either side of the court.

The lob serve is best executed by finding a spot on the front wall that, if struck with a serve of the proper speed and angle, continually results in an ideal or near-ideal shot. Having found the spot, the server need only aim for that spot each time. Spot serving will, in the long run, result in greater accuracy.

The arm motion should consist of an upward swing with a rigid wrist. The motion of the arm, rather than the wrist, will provide the impetus for the serve, because any movement of the wrist would tend to diminish the accuracy of the serve. Control of speed and location are most important for this shot.

The ball should be struck about chest high, with the arm extended and the knees slightly bent. The weight should be shifted from your back foot to the front foot during the course of the serve (Illus. 3-1, 2, 3).

After hitting the ball, continue with a follow-through that is smooth, not jerky.

• Z Serve

Like the lob serve, the Z serve can be used to keep an opponent in the back court. Depending on execution, the Z serve can be almost impossible to return.

The server can station himself in the middle of the service area or to either side, depending on where he wants the serve to go. The ball should be served against the front wall, rebound to the front side wall, then cross the court and, after bouncing on the floor, hit the back of the side wall. (Illus. 3-5). Ideally, it will come softly off the back side wall and die, or bounce unpredictably around the corner. It is imperative that the Z serve be hit accurately, with respect to speed as well as location. If the serve is hit short, it will bounce off the side wall near three-quarters court, leaving your opponent with an easy return. If the serve is hit too long, it will bounce off the back wall for a setup for your opponent.

One of the disadvantages of the Z serve is that it can be effectively dealt with by moving up to cut it off as it crosses the court to the back side wall. The server must use deception in his serves, keeping his opponent guessing. If his opponent begins cutting off the Z serve, the server should alter his choice of serves. The server can camouflage his serves by using a quick and consistent motion. (The lob serve is an exception.)

26

Illustration 3-5 *Low Z Serve*

The Z serve should be hit fairly hard with a forehand or backhand stroke. Usually it is hit with a forehand to either side of the court. By experimentation, a player can determine a spot on the wall that results in the proper angle for the path of the ball.

• Drive Serve (or V Serve)

The drive service is the most common serve in racquetball today. This is the serve that, if used properly, will cause ineffective service returns, giving you the third shot rekill. It is sometimes called the "V serve". It is also a power serve designed to make your opponent take a couple of quick steps before hitting the return. It should force your opponent to a side wall for what you hope will be a hurried and inaccurate return. (Illus. 3-6).

The drive serve usually is hit from the middle of the service area. It should hit the front wall from six to twelve inches above the floor. The ball should travel on a low, straight line toward the back side wall, near the corner. If it is hit hard enough, your opponent will be forced to hurry for a return. The server, however, must be careful not to flail the serve (hit it too hard) or it will come off the back wall for a setup.

Ideally, the drive serve will lose speed after hitting the back side wall and die in the corner. This serve can be dangerous if your opponent steps up and cuts the ball off before it hits the side wall.

Instead of aiming for deep back corner, try making the ball hit right past the short line in an angle to the back corner. It should cross over the short line so low and far away from your opponent that a return will be very difficult.

Remember, if hit too high, this serve will backfire. It is better to hit a short serve than a serve that would result in an easy setup for your opponent. In order to avoid the potential danger, the server should find a spot on the front wall for which to aim. Success with the drive serve, as with most serves, will increase if that spot is hit consistently. The percentage of accurate serves is higher with spot serving than it is with trying to guess at the angle.

• High Z Serve

The high Z serve is an excellent choice when a server is trying to achieve a ceiling ball return. This serve, if hit properly, will force your opponent to return the ball chest high and thus almost always result in a ceiling ball return.

The high Z serve is a variation of the garbage serve, except that it is hit at an angle which makes the execution and return slightly more difficult. Because of your location in the service zone, your opponent may be somewhat timid about rushing up and blasting the ball when it crosses the receiving line as he would have to hit the ball directly at you while you are still in the service box.

If you are serving to the left back corner, line up about five feet from the left wall (and vice versa on the right wall). Hit the ball at medium to light speed, with little wrist action, toward the right corner of the front wall. The stroke is easier to execute if you leave your arm extended and hit the ball with a smooth upward motion instead of the normal racquetball stroke. This will give you more accuracy and better placement of the ball. After the ball hits the front wall, it will carom to the side wall, then hit such that it travels crosscourt and strikes the floor a few feet behind the receiving line. Try to hit the ball about 12 to 15 feet high on the front wall. This height will allow the softly hit ball to arc down to the floor and bounce up instead of in a straight line towards the back court. This will force your opponent to hit the ball on the way up and about chest to shoulder high, resulting in the desired ceiling ball return (Illus. 3-7).

One possible disadvantage of this serve can occur if your opponent tries to rush the ball and take it on the bounce. Normally,

Illustration 3-6 *Drive Serve*

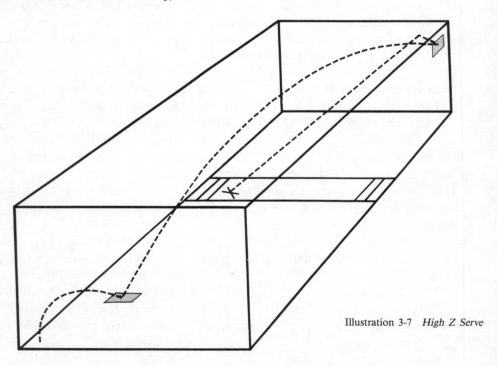

Illustration 3-7 *High Z Serve*

28

you are still moving out of the service box and could be caught by surprise and possibly hit by his return of service. On the other hand, if your opponent does not hit the ball before it strikes the back side wall, the ball should force him up against the back wall for a difficult shot. Practice this serve until you can hit it with complete accuracy and then use it regularly.

• Garbage Serve (or Low Lob Serve)

Each serve in racquetball is designed to force your opponent into a particular type of return or situation. There are offensive serves that force the action and usually bring about a quick gain or loss of the point. And then there are defensive serves, the most popular of which is the garbage serve or low lob serve.

The purpose of the garbage serve is simply to put the ball into play in a manner that makes a kill shot almost impossible. It is also custom-made for a player who thrives on ceiling ball rallies, since a ceiling ball is the safest return your opponent can make on a garbage serve.

The serve is similar to a lob serve, but without the high arc. The ball is hit between waist level and chest level, usually using a forehand, although a backhand can also be used. Aim for a spot on the front wall about eight feet from the floor. The ball should land about four feet from the short line, then bounce in a medium arc so that your opponent will be faced with a chest high shot (Illus. 3-8). Standing in the back court, swinging at chest level, your opponent will be practically incapable of a kill shot. His choice of shots is severely limited unless he wants to risk giving the server a distinct advantage on the next shot.

Angles on the garbage serve are not crucial, but speed is. A shallow shot will give your opponent the opportunity to charge ahead for a kill shot or a pass shot. An overly deep serve will bounce off the back wall for an easy return. Ideally, the serve should die at the base of the back wall, making a return impossible.

The garbage serve is the easiest to execute and, from appearances, the easiest to return. Appearances, though, can be deceiving. The serve is not fancy or difficult, so the less experienced player may think he can over-

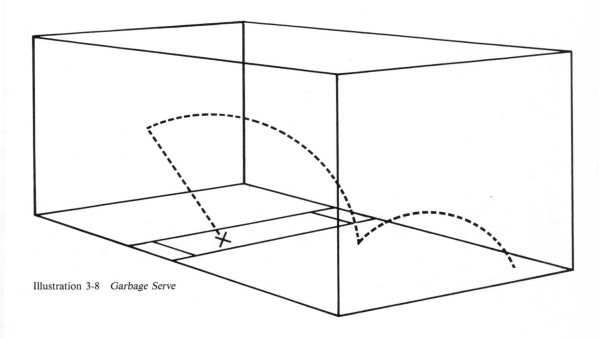

Illustration 3-8   *Garbage Serve*

Illustration 3-10   *Notice racquet height during ex-ecution of a garbage serve.*

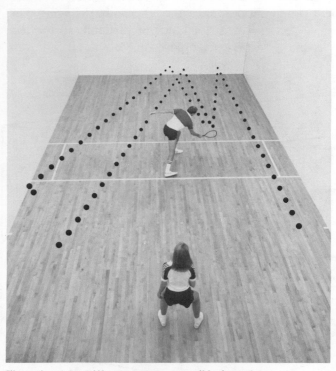

Illustration 3-9   *Different serves are possible from the center of the service zone!!*

power the return with a kill shot. If he tries such an attempt, be sure to get into position for a likely kill shot of your own, because the percentages are against him from the back court.

• Other Serve's

Two serves that are used infrequently, because of the difficulty in execution, are the *wallpaper serve* and the *crosscourt serve*. The wallpaper serve is intended to elicit a poor return by keeping the ball extremely close to the wall. The server positions himself near the wall and, with either a forehand or a backhand, aims for the front wall directly in front of him. The ball should rebound along a path as near to the wall as possible.

The only caution to observe, other than insuring that the ball does not hit the side wall and bounce out into the middle of the court, is to keep the ball from bouncing deep and off the back wall for a setup.

The crosscourt serve can produce an ace (a serve that completely alludes your opponent), but, as with most serves, it is difficult and it can backfire.

The server, standing in the middle of the service area, or just a step or two to one side, aims the serve crosscourt with the intention of hitting the side wall just past the short line and near the floor.

If the serve is excuted properly, the ball will practically roll out from the side wall, hopefully precluding a return. If it is executed improperly, the ball will either land shy of the short line for a second serve, or it will hit too high on the side wall and bounce into middle court for a plum (an easy setup).

SERVING STRATEGY

Before each serve, try to analyze the situation and decide which serve will be most effective. Your opponent's ability, his physical condition at the moment, the score, and the type of return you hope to elicit all

will be factors in your decision. If you want a ceiling ball, use a garbage serve. If a fast, running game is your perference, a low Z may be advisable.

Regardless of what serve you use, be sure not to use it to the exclusion of the other available serves. If your opponent knows what is coming, he has the jump on you. Change not only the serve, but also, its speed, your motion, or anything else to confuse your opponent.

The advantage is with you, the server. Do not forfeit it.

Illustration 3-11 *Ace Serve*

Have you ever noticed a basketball player shoot free throws? They always bounce the ball and do the same exact motions just prior to shooting the free throw. Try to develop this same habit while serving. It will give you more consistency and keep your opponent guessing which serve is coming next. Most serves are the same initial motion, so try to keep your opponent from guessing your serves.

Always try to serve from the middle of the court. Some top players try taking a few steps before hitting the serve. This is fine, just end up in the center of the service zone. You have a full ten seconds to serve once in the zone, so there is plenty of time to think about which serve to hit. Be sure to focus on the right spot on the front wall and know which shot to execute.

COURT POSITION

Moving into position after serving decreases your opponent's chances of making a winning return. If, for instance, you serve from the middle of the service zone and the ball goes deep to the corner toward your opponent's backhand, you should take several steps toward your opponent. Watch him as he makes his return. You should be in a position for almost any shot he hits. (Illus. 3-12).

From his position in his backhand corner, his choice of high percentage shots consists of a ceiling ball and a pass shot. You are now practically in the back court, so you should have no trouble with a ceiling ball. Another step or two backward will give you

position for the ceiling ball. If he tries a pass shot, you should be able to reach it fairly easily since you are in shallow back court. Only a lazy player is susceptible to a pass shot when they are in the back court.

If your opponent attempts a kill shot from the corner, you should not be vulnerable unless he hits a rollout. Otherwise, you are near enough to the front court to move up and put the ball away.

Moving a couple of steps toward your opponent after you serve is good percentage racquetball, since most of your opponent's returns are designed to land in the back court. If you move back immediately after hitting the ball, you probably will not be as rushed on your next shot.

Some players try to shoot (go for a winner) from the back court regardless of your position. As soon as you realize this, forego the backward steps and begin to anticipate where the returns are going. When you have established where he likes to shoot, begin to move there while he is hitting. If you do not, you may be too late even if you know where the ball is going.

Many players make the mistake of

Illustration 3-12 *Position to take after service.*

watching the ball on the front wall after they serve. Absolutely do not watch the front wall after serving. This can be dangerous. As you await the next shot, your opponent is watching the ball and may unintentionally strike you with their racquet while moving to the ball. You know that the ball will eventually be hit by your opponent, so try to watch them set up. After serving, turn your head and concentrate on your opponent's body and feet for a hint of the type of return he will make. It should improve your anticipation and help your reaction time. (Note: Don't watch your opponent hit the ball—turn back towards the front wall just as they begin to hit the ball.) The techniques and strategy for return of serve are somewhat more advanced and are discussed in Chapter Five.

Illustration 3-13   *The ready position.*

Illustration 4-1   Illustration 4-2

 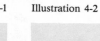

Illustration 4-3   Illustration 4-4

An important key to the backhand kill shot is to use plenty of body motion during the execution. Notice the stretching of the legs as the backhand is performed.

chapter 4

THE SHOTS OF RACQUETBALL

Of the various shots in racquetball, some will be used more than others. Some will be used for offensive purposes, some for defensive purposes. Some will be rather easy to learn, others very difficult.

Some shots can be used in almost any situation, some must be used only in rare situations. Some shots will be used extensively by some individuals, and practically ignored by others.

It will be stressed in this chapter, and in the chapter on strategy, that each player must determine the shots at which he is most skilled, and which shots are most suited for his style of play.

Understandably, most shots are offensive because, after all, the object of the game is to score points. But it is still imperative in today's racquetball to develop your defensive shots.

DEFENSIVE SHOTS

Before the ceiling ball was introduced in 1969, racquetball was more or less a one-dimensional game. A premium was placed on kill shots, pass shots and overall power. The ceiling ball, a defensive shot, revolutionized the game because it allowed a player whose strong points were patience and control to compete successfully with the power players.

Developing a ceiling shot is comparable to a pitcher cultivating a good curve ball to complement his fast ball. With only a fast ball, regardless of how good it is, a pitcher will not be successful. He must have a reasonably adequate curve ball. The same hitters who thrive on fast balls are sometimes the ones who are baffled by curves.

So it is with racquetball, whereby a player with an excellent kill shot or power game can be confused and frustrated by throwing him a curve in the form of a ceiling ball.

However, with the advent of today's fast racquetball, you must also have an excellent low-kill game to complement your defensive shots. To rely solely on your ceiling and pass game may tend to tire your opponent at times, but be assured you will lose in the long run. You must be able to shoot the ball to win in racquetball today. But to compete with a power hitter, it is imperative that you keep him away from the front and middle court, and there is no better method available than the ceiling ball.

There is not a top-level player in racquetball who is less than adept in the use of the ceiling ball. Even if the slow, control game is not well-suited for a particular player and he decides not to use it as a weapon, he must at least become skillful enough with the shot so that it is not successfully used as a weapon against him.

Because the ceiling ball has gained such widespread acceptance, it must become part of your repertoire.

• Forehand Ceiling Ball

As simple as it may appear to an observer, the ceiling ball is not easily executed with accuracy. But like all shots, it can be practiced until accuracy becomes routine.

The forehand ceiling ball motion is more common than the backhand and can also be more quickly mastered. The shot is almost identical to the overhead smash in tennis, yet even some experienced players do not use quite the correct motion. To learn the proper technique, or to cure bad habits, several principles should be observed.

To begin, grasp the racquet with the regular forehand grip. As in a tennis serve or as in throwing a baseball, the arm motion should be directly over the shoulder of your swinging arm. The arm is bent as you begin the swing, but before contact with the ball, as your arm reaches the top of the swing, it should straighten so that it is fully extended upon impact. A mild snap of the wrist just before contact will help propel the ball, as will a moderate follow-through across your body (Illus. 4-6, 7, 8).

An improper forehand ceiling ball swing often leads to the painful arm condition sometimes known as tennis elbow. I played for two years with a constant ache in my elbow and after talking with numerous doctors and other experts, I was advised to discontinue playing. Eventually I discovered that the pain was the result of my ceiling ball swing. I was striking the ball out away to the side and behind my body rather than directly over my shoulder, thereby putting an added and injurious strain on my elbow. The motion I was using was forcing my elbow and shoulder to absorb the shock of impact with the ball.

Another advantage to be gained from hitting the ball overhead, as opposed to out to the side, is court position. Once the ball is hit and traveling in a downward arc, a player who is hitting the ball three to four feet over his shoulder will be able to stand several feet farther forward in the court than the player who must wait for the ball to descend to a level even with his head or shoulder. And sometimes those one or two steps are the difference between wining and losing a point.

The path of the ceiling ball begins, obviously, at the racquet and continues to the ceiling, striking from about two to five feet from the front wall. After rebounding off the front wall, the ball lands near mid-

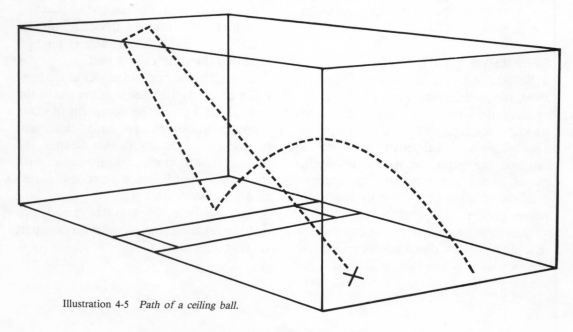

Illustration 4-5 *Path of a ceiling ball.*

Illustration 4-6

Illustration 4-7

Illustration 4-8   *Hold the racquet in a ready position, hit the ball high, and follow-through across your body for the forehand ceiling ball.*

dle court and bounces in a high arc toward the back wall (Illus. 4-5).

A ball hit too near the middle of the ceiling will end up in middle court, rather than in back court, thereby defeating your purpose and allowing your opponent to attempt a high percentage kill shot or pass shot. In addition, a shot with too much velocity will bounce high off the back wall for a possible setup.

Occasionally you will encounter an opponent who likes to cutoff a ceiling ball in middle court. To minimize the effectiveness of such a maneuver, aim the ball to the side of the court opposite him. If they are exceptionally quick, and will get to the ball anyway, at least you will find out from which part of the court they are least likely to hit a successful shot. Remember, also, to move up quickly to take advantage of a possible, missed kill shot. If your opponent has moved up into front or middle court for the cutoff, they will be vulnerable to a pass shot.

Illustration 4-9   Illustration 4-10

Illustration 4-11 *Keep the racquet away from your body while hitting the backhand ceiling ball.*

• Backhand Ceiling Ball

The backhand ceiling ball stroke seems difficult and unorthodox to most beginning players, primarily because it is a motion that they are rarely called upon to use in most other sports. Actually, the backhand ceiling ball motion is more natural than the forehand and less of a strain on the arm.

The backhand is not hit directly over the shoulder, as is the forehand, but at a 45 degree angle away from the body. For optimum power, keep the racquet fairly high.

A good, consistent backhand ceiling ball stroke is acquired only through extended practice.

Things to remember about the backhand ceiling ball:

(1) Have the racquet in position to swing before the ball arrives in the hitting area. Very important!

(2) Use the regular backhand grip.

(3) The path of the arm should be to the side, but fairly high (Illus. 4-9, 10, 11).

(4) As you swing, shift your weight from the back leg to the front leg.

(5) Step forward, not backward, as you swing for better power and accuracy.

(6) After hitting the ball, move up a few steps for better position. Watch your opponent and anticipate his next shot.

• The Z Ball

A primarily defensive shot, the Z ball is used infrequently because of its difficulty and the necessity for the element of surprise.

The purpose of the shot, first of all, is to move your opponent into the back court, although it can be an offensive shot if it is hit to perfection. By the same token, if the Z ball is hit poorly, it will give your opponent an easy shot.

The Z ball is similar to the high Z serve with respect to the path of the ball from racquet to high front wall, to side wall, to back side wall (Illus. 4-12). The Z ball can be attempted from anywhere on the court, but it is more likely to be successful if used in the front court. The shot requires a fair amount of power to be effective.

Somewhat similar to the high Z serve (Chapter 3), the front wall to side wall combination will impart a spin on the ball that, if the angles and speed are correct, causes it to come off the back side wall parallel to the back wall, making a return extremely difficult. Careless execution of the Z ball will result in a shot that misses the back side wall entirely, or one that hits the side wall in the vicinity of mid-court.

To attempt a Z ball from the back court requires tremendous power and, as such, produces a greater margin for error. It is better strategy to use it during a fast rally in the front court, perhaps to change the pattern of play. If you choose to hit a Z

ball from the back court, be sure to move immediately to the middle of the court to avoid being pinned in the back court by your own shot (a Z ball from the back court will usually return to the area of its origin).

• Around-The-Wall Ball

An infrequently used defensive shot that is used to move your opponent out of the middle court area and into the back court is the around-the-wall ball (Illus. 4-13).

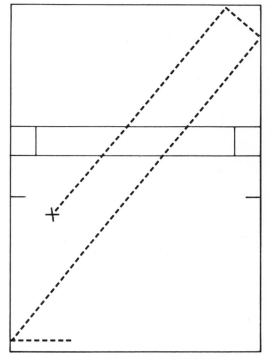

Illustration 4-12 Path of Z Ball

The only difference between it and the Z ball is that the around-the-wall ball hits the side wall first, rather than the front wall.

Hit the ball, with medium velocity, toward a point high on the side wall. The ball will rebound high to the front wall in the corner and cross the court toward the opposite back corner. By using the proper speed and angle, you can prevent the ball from bouncing off the back wall for a setup.

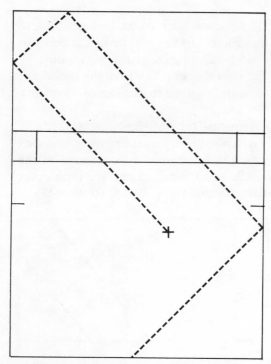
Illustration 4-13 *Path of Around-The-Wall Ball.*

This shot, like its Z ball counterpart, is dangerous if not hit accurately. The shot can be directed toward either side wall, although you probably will be better off hitting to the wall that will force your opponent to use a backhand.

OFFENSIVE SHOTS

In nearly every sport there is a shot or play whose purpose and procedure is similar to racquetball's kill shot. In baseball, a hitter swinging for the fences is attempting a type of kill shot. In certain situations, with the right player, it is advisable to go for the home run, despite the fact that the chances for a strike out are increased.

In football, the long pass, or bomb, is a kill shot in that it can result in a quick score. Again, the chances of an interception are better, but it is a calculated risk that should be taken in certain situations.

The risk inherent in a racquetball kill shot is the chance that it will not be hit accurately and consequently will give your opponent

an opportunity to do what you were unable to do—hit the ball so that a return is all but impossible.

The best kill shot is one that results in a flat "rollout," whereby the ball simply rolls out from the front wall without bouncing. Kill shots can be attempted by hitting the front wall first or hitting the side wall to the front wall (pinch shot), or by hitting the front wall and then the side wall.

A kill shot is more likely to be successful from certain areas of the floor than from others. A player must discover these areas and learn his limitations in order to know when not to try a kill shot, as well as when to try one.

Different types of kill shots are listed below:
1. Front wall kills (down-the-wall & V kill)
2. Pinch shot (sidewall to front wall)
3. Front wall-side wall kill
4. Off-the-back-wall kill
5. Drop shot
6. Reverse pinch shot
7. Splat shot

• Front Wall Kill

A very common shot, the front wall kill can be hit with either the forehand or the backhand. Facing either side wall, you should attempt to get as low as possible, with knees bent. The lower the racquet connects with the ball, the better the chances for a rollout. By stretching out and keeping the body low to the floor, you will be able to hit the ball close to the floor, giving the ball a low flight toward the wall. (Illus. 4-18). A kill shot that is attempted at knee level or higher, because of laziness or poor judgment, will likely jump up after hitting the wall to give your opponent an easy kill shot.

Remember to have the racquet in ready position as the ball enters the hitting area, and then keep your eyes on the ball throughout the execution of the shot.

Illustration 4-14   Illustration 4-15

Illustration 4-16   Illustration 4-17
Randy shows proper form for the low forehand kill. Notice how low he is to the floor.

The V kill is hit at an angle wide enough so that if the ball hits too high on the front wall it will result in a V Pass (pg. 47) instead of the intended kill shot (Illus. 4-19).

The shot can be tried from anywhere on the court, but the chances for success are greater from the center court. It is usually unwise to use the front wall kill if your opponent is directly in front of you.

There are several choices of front wall kill

Illustration 4-18   *Down-the-Wall Front Wall Kill.*

shots. First, the *down-the-wall* kill is effective when your opponent is either behind or to one side of you. The down-the-wall kill is one of the best shots in the game. It is usually tried on the service return or if you are on a side wall and your opponent is in the center court. Simply aim the down-the-wall kill as close to a side wall as possible, being careful not to hit the wall (Illus. 4-18). One advantage of the shot when hit too high is it might result in a nice pass shot. A disadvantage of this shot is that it is very difficult to keep the ball from hitting a side wall and ending up in center court for a plum ball (an easy return) for your oppo-

nent. So keep it low and down-the-line and you should experience excellent results. A *V kill* or *crosscourt kill* shot is also an excellent choice (Illus. 4-19). It is a good choice to use when your opponent is next to you and would be too close for a down-the-wall kill.

• The Pinch Shot
(Side Wall to Front Wall)

The pinch shot need not be hit quite as low as the front wall kill because the two-wall combination will slow the ball down.

The pinch shot should hit the side wall anywhere from just above the floor to 18″ high and two to four feet from the front wall, then carom to the front wall, and then bounce off at an angle toward the opposite side wall, rather than toward the middle of the court (Illus. 4-20). The pinch is an excellent shot to use, but try not to overuse

Illustration 4-19   *V Kill*

this kill. Good opponents will anticipate excessive use and play closer to the front wall and try to pick these shots up for a rekill.

The ball should be hit moderately hard most of the time, but a soft pinch shot will offer a change of pace and may fool your opponent.

In learning the pinch shot, a player probably should begin by positioning his feet toward the spot on the side wall where the

you if used in the right situations.

If you are on the right side of the court, aim for the front wall at a point no higher than thigh level. Ideally, the ball will rebound to the right side wall near the floor, or at least low enough to make a return difficult (illus. 4-21).

Illustration 4-20 *Pinch Shot.*

Always hit to pinch on the side of the court your opponent is near, so the ball will end up going away from your opponent after hitting the front wall.

ball will hit. With practice a player will be able to hit the shot without positioning his feet in the direction of the shot, making it possible to confuse the opponent by facing one way and hitting to another. For beginners, it is probably easier to learn the safe, dependable way first and then add more advanced modifications later.

• The Front Wall-Side Wall Kill

The front wall-side wall kill is a good shot to try when your opponent is in back court. To keep the ball out of the center court area, it is best to hit to the same side of the court you are on. The front wall-side wall is not a difficult shot to make and it will score for

Illustration 4-21 *Front Wall-Side Wall Kill.*

The deeper your opponent's position, the better the chance of beating him with a front wall-side wall kill. If he is in front court, he is in good position to retrieve your shot and execute a pinch shot of his own. It should be mentioned that a crosscourt front wall-side wall kill likely will end up in mid-court if not hit perfectly. By keeping the ball on your side of the court, you can hit a somewhat inaccurate shot and still make it difficult for your opponent to return.

• The Off-The-Back Wall Kill

Players often will make the mistake of hitting a shot so hard, or a ceiling ball so deep, that it bounces off the back wall, giving your opponent an opportunity for an

43

Illustration 4-22

Illustration 4-23   Illustration 4-24
Having the racquet in a ready position before striking the ball will help perfect off-the-back wall shots.

off-the-back-wall kill. If you play an opponent who has a habit of flailing (hitting the ball hard without regard to where it is going), be sure your off-the-back wall game is sharp.

Footwork and coordination are extremely important with this shot because of the necessity for judging where and how fast the ball will come off the back wall. The ball will rebound shallow and slowly if it hits the floor before hitting the back wall. If, however, it comes off the front wall or ceiling and hits the back wall without first hitting the floor, the ball will jump suddenly out into the center court area.

It requires quick feet and quick thinking to, first, determine where the ball will end up after hitting the back wall, and then, to get there. If you are there waiting for the ball with your racquet in the ready position, you will be able to get low and hit the ball low, which is required in all kill shots. (Illus. 4-22, 23, 24).

Only with practice and experience is a player able to hit kill shots effectively off the back wall. Nevertheless, it is a basic shot that must be learned in order to play winning racquetball.

• **The Drop Shot**

The drop shot is classified as a kill shot, even though it seems a bunt in comparison to the home runs already discussed.

When you are in front court and your opponent is in back court, the drop shot is an effective strategem. It should be hit, or more precisely, punched with a slight swing of the arm and a cocked wrist. If hit very softly, it will "drop" into the front wall near the floor and barely dribble out into shallow front court (Illus. 4-31).

It is a finesse shot that will backfire if not hit accurately or in the right situation. Since the ball only hits one surface (the front wall) there is a good chance it will bounce out for a setup if not hit softly enough and low enough. Similarly, if your opponent is not deep in back court, he will be able to run forward for a return, in which case you will be susceptible to all sorts of pass shots.

• **Reverse Pinch**

The reverse pinch is a shot that your forehand hits to the left side wall with a pinch shot or vice versa with a back hand. It is an option if your opponent is next to the left side wall (Illus. 4-25). Remember this shot has to be hit hard as backward spin is imparted on the ball for which you need more velocity than with a regular pinch. In average play, a V kill would probably be more appropriate.

• **Splat**

This is a new shot used exclusively for advanced power players. You hit the ball hard about two feet from a side wall which should impart spin. The ball shoots to the front wall and spins somewhat parallel with the front wall (Illus. 4-26). When hit properly, it is not only discouraging for your opponent but impossible to return. Probably a better shot for beginners is a down-the-wall kill.

PASS SHOTS

If there is any disadvantage to a perfect kill shot, it may be that your opponent can only watch, probably with some admiration, as the ball rolls out from the wall. He does not use much energy watching.

Rarely will your opponent stand and watch as you hit a passing shot. More likely, he will exert himself and, hopefully, tire himself running after the ball. Naturally, it is better to get the point than to merely run your opponent, but with the proper use of pass shots, you can do both.

There are three different variations of a pass shot.
1. Down-the-wall pass
2. V pass
3. Crosscourt pass

Illustration 4-25 *Reverse Pinch Shot*

Illustration 4-26 *Splat Shot*

• Down-The-Wall Pass

The down-the-wall pass is best used when you are on one side of the court and your opponent is on the other. A firm shot that rebounds along the wall nearest you will be difficult for your opponent to retrieve.

The forehand down-the-wall pass is hit with the racquet away from the body and just out from your forward foot. The shot should be hit hard enough that your opponent does not cut it off at mid-court, but softly enough that it does not rebound off the back wall.

The backhand down-the-wall pass is

• V Pass

Probably the most commonly used pass shot is the V pass. When you are on one side of the court and your opponent is on the same side or in mid-court, a good, hard V pass will give him trouble. It is a simple crosscourt shot that travels in a "V" path. (Illus. 4-28).

The V pass, which can be used with either the forehand or backhand, should be hit with more speed than the down-the-wall pass. It is an effective alternative to the kill shot, and it is best used when your opponent is in front of you expecting a kill shot.

Illustration 4-27 *Backhand Down-The-Wall Pass*

Illustration 4-28   *V Pass*

perhaps one of the most effective shots in racquetball. Always try to hit this shot when you are 3-8 feet from the side wall and your opponent is on your forehand side. Try to angle the ball so that once it hits the front wall and after it hits the floor, it slices into the back side wall, before it hits the back-wall (Illus. 4-27). Always angle your pass shots towards the back side wall to slow the ball down and hopefully stop the ball from coming off the back wall for an easy setup.

After a certain amount of practice, you will be able to hit the right angle almost instinctively. As mentioned, the V pass should be hit hard, but do not sacrifice accuracy by overhitting the ball. Use a smooth, even stroke.

The V pass can be used from nearly every position on the court and, consequently, the angle will change with each different position. Since the angle of your shot is dependent on both your position and your opponent's position, you may find it difficult to practice the shot by yourself.

By enlisting the help of your opponent before a pickup game (a casual "just for fun" game) and stationing him at different positions on the court, you can practice the different angles for each position, thereby facilitating the visualization of the angles during a match.

The V pass deserves extra concentration during practice and actual play because of its effectiveness and value as an offensive

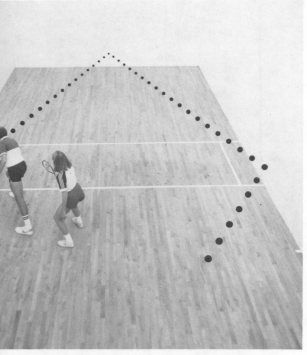

Illustration 4-29 *Crosscourt Pass*

weapon. It is not the most difficult shot to hit, but it should be used with discretion against an extremely quick player who may cut off the shot before it crosses the court. If you are in backcourt at the time, they will have an easy kill.

Another advantage of the shot is that it can be hit from practically any height, although the path of the shot should be kept as low as possible.

• **Crosscourt Pass**

Now, the crosscourt pass. Most players do not make the correct distinction between a V pass and a crosscourt pass. The crosscourt pass is simply a wide-angle V pass that hits the side wall before hitting the floor and it is one of the best shots in the game. You do not have to be super accurate, nor have tremendous power, to effectively use this shot. In my opinion, it is more effective than the V pass because it is harder for your opponent to cut the ball off and it is less likely to rebound off the back wall because the side wall will slow its velocity (Illus. 4-29).

Really try to learn this shot. It is very effective when hit wide. It will tend to rebound off the side wall very fast and therefore squeeze your opponent. If it is not hit wide enough, you then have to settle for a V pass, which is not a bad choice. It is easy to hit with either your forehand or your backhand. Try to remember to use a level stroke, not a pendulum swing, to keep the flight of the ball level. This will help keep the ball off the back wall. Use the same type of drill as described for the V pass to practice this shot.

THE OVERHEAD KILL AND DRIVE

In the pecking order of racquetball shots, the overhead kill will not be ranked among the most effective or most valuable. If used sparingly, however, it can be called upon with some success.

The overhead kill is a low percentage shot because of the difficulty in execution. Some top tournament players use it extensively with good results, but only because they have worked at perfecting it.

Taking into consideration the earlier discussion of kill shots, the name "overhead kill" seems to be a contradiction in terms. It has been stressed that you should get as low as possible to hit most kill shots. That, obviously, is impossible on an overhead kill.

The shot is made with an overhead, ceiling ball-type motion from the back court, which makes anything approaching a flat rollout extremely difficult.

The most opportune time to use the overhead kill is during a ceiling ball rally, when the repetition and monotony of ceiling ball after ceiling ball has caused your opponent to lapse into a state of daydreaming. An overhead kill in that situation, even if it is slightly inaccurate, has a good chance of catching him off guard.

The shot should never be attempted when your opponent is in front court. Unless you hit a perfect rollout, which is unlikely from your back court position, he probably will retrieve your shot and end the point with a drop shot.

Like the ceiling ball, the overhead kill should be hit with a straight extension of the arm, using limited wrist action. It should be aimed toward a corner, preferably at a side wall first. If hit properly, with medium speed, the ball will hit the side wall near the floor and rebound off the front wall in a rollout. The shot resembles a pinch shot in its side wall-front wall combination (Illus. 4-30).

The overhead drive is not nearly as risky as the overhead kill and, as such, may be used more frequently. Its primary purpose is to keep your opponent in the back court. If, during a ceiling ball rally, your opponent moves up into middle court after each shot, you may even be able to pass him for a winner. Depending on his position, your drive may take the form of a V pass or a down-the-wall pass from a back court position.

The overhead drive is hit with the same stroke as the ceiling ball and overhead kill. It should hit the front wall from two feet to four feet high and with enough speed to either pass your opponent or drive him into deep back court. By keeping the ball low, you will be better able to prevent it coming off the back wall for a setup.

PRACTICE—PRACTICE—PRACTICE

The following chart is a practice schedule listing each shot, the number of repetitions suggested, and the area of the court in which the shot should be practiced. If the schedule is followed as described here, using the

Illustration 4-30 *Overhead Kill-Ball hits low in both corners, rolls out from the wall, and then dies.*

49

forehand and backhand for each shot, approximately one hour will be required. The number of repetitions may be changed as desired. Those players who wish to develop their skills and improve steadily should practice according to this schedule several times a week. Those players who wish to become top tournament players should practice even more often and with more repetitions.

Illustration 4-31 *Randy shows the proper drop shot form. The ball 'drops' against the front wall and dribbles out into shallow front court.*

ONE HOUR PRACTICE SCHEDULE

SHOTS	NO. OF REPETITIONS	AREA OF COURT TO PRACTICE SHOT FROM
Defensive:		
Ceiling Ball	75	Back
Z Ball	10	All Areas
Around-The-Wall Ball	10	All Areas
Offensive:		
Down-The-Wall Kill	10	Along Side Walls
V Kill (or Crosscourt Kill)	10	Near a Side Wall
Pinch	25	Middle and Back
Front Wall-Side Wall Kill	25	Middle and Back
Drop Shot	20	Front
Overhead Kill	15	Middle and Back
Overhead Drive	15	Middle and Back
Front Wall Kill (Straight-In Kill)	10	Middle and Back
Off-The-Back Wall Kill	10	Back
Passes:		
Down-The-Wall Pass	25	All Areas
V Pass	15	All Areas
Crosscourt Pass	15	All Areas
Serves:		
Lob Serve	10	Service Zone
Z Serve	10	Service Zone
Drive Serve (or V Serve)	10	Service Zone
High Z Serve	10	Service Zone
Garbage Serve (or Low Lob Serve)	10	Service Zone
Crosscourt Serve	10	Service Zone

Illustration 5-1   *An accurate low drive serve can result in a weak service return.*

Illustration 5-2   *Front wall-side wall kill.*

chapter 5

ALL ABOUT STRATEGY AND A TOURNAMENT MATCH

Strategy becomes increasingly important as a player becomes increasingly skillful at racquetball. Strategy is fairly useless without skills, but so are skills without strategy.

Put simply, strategy is a personal game plan that takes advantage of a player's strengths and his opponent's weaknesses. In racquetball, it includes everything from preparation for a tournament, to the direction of a passing shot, to when to call time out.

Because of all the variables in a match, your strategy should never be exactly the same for any two matches. You may change, your opponent may change, the situation may change. You may be playing a control player or a kill player. Your strategy will change depending on your physical conditioning during a match. It will change as the score changes.

Before any strategy can be implemented, a player has to be able to recognize and evaluate each situation. He must be able to assimilate all the variables and then formulate a course of action.

SIZING UP YOUR OPPONENT

Since your opponent is as much a part of your strategy as your own game, try to find out as much about him as possible before your match. In a tournament situation, you will be aware of who you will be playing. If possible, find out when he plays in a previous round and go watch his match. It should give you a good indication of his strengths and weaknesses.

It helps a great deal to know what to look for as you watch. You may want to bring along a pen and paper to jot down some things about his game. In what part of the court does he seem to concentrate his play? Does he move effectively to the right or left, or both? After a hard run to the side wall, what type of shot does he usually hit? Will he try a kill shot from the back court to avoid hitting a ceiling ball?

Every player has a style that manifests itself in the type of shots he hits and does not hit, in how much running he does, in how fiercely he competes, and so on. By watching your opponent for a short time, you should be able to analyze his style and begin to construct a game plan.

If you do not have a chance to observe your opponent, ask other people about him. They may not be able to tell you anything more than the fact that he is right-handed, but at least you will know more about him than you did before.

Your ultimate strategy will depend on how he plays you. Watch him as he warms up. If he stands in one position for several minutes and hits rollouts from 39 feet, he is obviously good at the shot.

Use the first few points of a match for experimentation. "Feel him out," as they say. Try a variety of serves to see which cause him the most trouble. He inevitably will return some serves better than others, so you had better find out which they are early in the match. When he adapts to one serve, switch to another.

As your opponent begins serving, watch him carefully. Usually his serve will be designed to force you into a particular type of return and, in effect, play his type of game. How well you avoid letting him dictate the tempo will be crucial to the match.

Continue analyzing and observing. Does he tend to give you easy shots by hitting ceiling balls so hard that they come off the back wall? If so, use garbage serves or any other serves or shots that force him into a ceiling ball rally. If he does not move into position for a backhand well, flood his backhand area with pass shots.

Every player has weaknesses relative to the rest of his game. The sooner you detect them, the sooner you can adapt your strategy to take advantage of them.

ANALYZING YOUR OWN GAME ("Know Thyself")

Long before you begin to think about your opponent and his game, you must come to an understanding with yourself about your own game. What are your capabilities? What can you do and what can you not do? What kind of shape are you in?

Answer those questions and you will have laid the foundation for your strategy. Determine before the match whether you can hit a kill shot from the back court or a high Z serve. In other words, decide before the match which shots you can make and cannot make. High percentage shots for one person may be low percentage shots for someone else.

Decide before the match if you can compete in a fast, running game, or if you would be better off in a controlled, ceiling ball-type game. Find out the areas of the court in which you feel most comfortable so that you can concentrate your game in those areas.

If you can hit winners consistently from

only one spot on the court, it should be your strategy to force the action into that area. Practice sessions and practice games, not tournament matches, are for finding out about yourself. Know what you can do before the match starts.

SERVING STRATEGY

Having the serve is an advantage and should be treated as such. Anyone who merely puts the ball into play without thinking ahead is forfeiting that advantage.

Even if you choose not to resort to an offensive serve, the serve you use should at least force your opponent into a type of return that helps you proceed with your game plan. If you are capable of hitting offensive serves, you will find that an ace or two will boost your confidence as well as your point total.

Theoretically, your serve should play two purposes. It ought to create difficulty for your opponent in returning the ball, and it should force him into the type of return you desire. In serving, take advantage of his weaknesses, whether they be backhands, shots on the run, overheads, etc., and then try to anticipate where his return will go. The more difficulty you cause him in returning your serve, the more bad returns he will hit and the more you will be in control of the match.

If you like to hit ceiling balls, your opponent can be coaxed into that type of game by using certain serves. If you prefer to be aggressive in the front court, force him into a difficult return, hoping he will be impatient and make an ill-advised kill attempt. Nine times out of ten, an impatient player will ignore the percentages and shoot if you can entice him with what appears to be a setup.

To entice him, give him a serve at about waist level. If he tries a kill shot, you are then able to move quickly into front court for an easy plum. (Your opponent will probably

Illustration 5-4 *Down-the-wall pass from return of service.*

Illustration 5-3 *Look at opponent before serving.*

still be in back court admiring what he thought would be a winner.)

Of course, if he can really smash a waist-high serve, you will have to change tactics, perhaps to a lob serve or a low Z serve.

In any case, it is a good idea to mix up your serves to prevent your opponent from anticipating. Try to be as sneaky and as noncommittal as possible. Practice the different serves until you are able to go to the service area, plant your foot approximately in the same place every time, drop the ball in a consistent manner and swing the racquet the same way for nearly all the serves you will be using.

It may be difficult to swing the same way each time, but even if the swing changes to some degree, you will be able to keep your opponent guessing with a quick motion.

For most serves, it is best to position yourself in the middle of the service area so that you will be only steps away from either side of the court. Remember, from center court you can execute most of the serves, giving you more choices.

A player who serves from near the side wall is also somewhat vulnerable to a down-the-wall pass on the opposite side. Serving from the side is not discouraged, as long as the server is quick to move back into position and guard any unprotected areas.

RETURN OF SERVE

If the serve is such an imporant element in your strategy, then the return of serve must be equally important for your opponent. It may be the most important shot in the game.

The easiest way for the server to score is on an errant return of serve. For reasons that defy explanation, a surprising number of points in a match are won and lost on service returns.

If you are returning serve, your opponent will be trying to force you into a particular type of return. As a counter tactic, you

Illustration 5-5 *Notice how Larry concentrates during a return of a lob serve.*

should try to hit the return that puts him in a difficult position. That does not mean you have to shoot on return of serve. Too many inexperienced players lose matches because of their insistence on attempting shots out of their range of capability. Consider the odds and know what you can and can not do when returning serve.

Probably the safest return, and one that, at least from an offensive standpoint, negates the server's advantage, is the ceiling ball. It enables you to move into the center court while your opponent moves into the back court. Even if your opponent is an excellent server, your chances of making an effective ceiling ball return are good.

For beginners, there are few instances when it is advisable to shoot on a return of serve. The percentages simply do not favor consistent success from a back court position. Just as in casino gambling, you may win your first few trips to the table, but chances are you will walk out broke and your confidence gone at the end of the night.

Patience is a virtue not easily acquired when it comes to returning serve—the temptation to go for a winner is, at times, overwhelming. Deliver yourself from temptation by considering the long-term chances of winning. Unless you have an obvious setup, opt for a ceiling ball return or a pass shot.

Of course, some players of exceptional ability can shoot consistently when returning serve. And even for those players of lesser ability, it is wise to shoot a poor serve every so often (maybe one out of eight serves) to break a pattern and keep your opponent guessing.

In time, you will develop the confidence to shoot in back court with your opponent in center court. Practice by yourself to develop these shots. At higher levels of play, this is a common shot; however, it should only be tried when your opponent has given you a setup in back court that you have the confidence to hit as a bottom board (just above the floor) kill shot.

Two excellent service returns are the down-the-wall pass and the crosscourt pass. The crosscourt pass, a common shot for returning a serve, is especially effective when your opponent is moving to front court in anticipation of a kill. Anytime he is in front court, you should be able to beat him with a down-the-wall pass or a crosscourt pass. (Illus. 5-4, 6).

With most serves going to either corner, the V pass and down-the-wall pass often are

Illustration 5-6 *A crosscourt pass from return is an excellent choice.*

effective as alternatives to the ceiling ball.

The down-the-wall pass, while not as easy to execute as the crosscourt pass, is a good shot to try if you are on one side of the court and the server is on the other. Be sure to avoid hitting the side wall, which would either send the ball into middle court, or slow it up enough to allow your opponent to retrieve it. It is imperative that you hit the ball hard enough to prevent him from cutting it off in center court. (He would have the entire front court to shoot for.)

Cutting off your opponent's serves is often good strategy, especially if the serves are consistently landing and dying in the corner. Always move up and cut off a serve rather than allow it to enter the corner. While receiving service, there is a rule you need to be aware of: once a ball is served you cannot cross the receiving line until the ball has either struck the floor past the short line or has passed the receiving line on the fly.

If it is obvious that the serve will go deep and rebound off the back wall, allow it to do so. If there is any doubt, however, do not take a chance. In an important match, against a good opponent, you can assume that most of his serves will be aimed for the corner. And if your kill shot has gone cold, do not sit back and give up more points waiting for it to get hot. Move up to cut off the serve or try other returns.

Although the server has the advantage from the beginning, you can reduce or eliminate it by making a good return. Play the percentages. Make him earn his points.

COURT POSITION

Most players, even good tournament players, will tend to play better or worse in some areas of the court than in others.

You will often find a fast, aggressive player roaming the front court. A slow player with a penchant for ceiling balls will spend a lot of time in the back court. A

good control player may choose to occupy the center court area if he is equally effective in front court and back court.

Skilled racquetball players have well-rounded games and can perform well in each area, but rarely will a player not have a preference for one part of the court. Find out his preference and then concentrate your game in the other parts of the court.

• Front Court

There are several strategies for play in the front court, which is defined as the area between the front wall and the short line.

Every shot in the front court area is dictated by your position and the position of

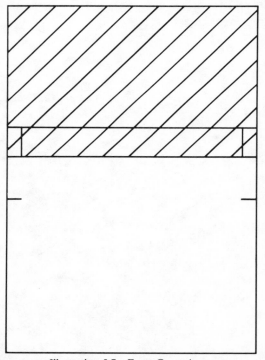

Illustration 5-7 *Front Court Area.*

your opponent. For example, if you have a forehand shot in the right front court and your opponent is in the middle of, or in front of, the service area, your best shot is a

Illustration 5-8 *In this situation, a down-the-wall pass is the best shot.*

Illustration 5-9 *Remember to hit a pinch shot to the side of the court your opponent is on. This will cause the ball to move away from your opponent after the ball hits the two walls.*

down-the-wall pass on the right side (Illus. 5-11).

You may attempt a kill to the right corner in that situation, but it may result in a hinder call if you end up in the path between the ball and your opponent. (Hinders will be discussed in detail in the next chapter.)

If you are in the right front court and your opponent is behind the receiving line, a down-the-wall pass would be a poor choice. From a deep position, such a shot would be fairly easily cut off. Instead, try a front wall kill or a pinch shot if your opponent is too deep to move up for a return or a hinder call (Illus. 5-9).

With you in the right front court and your opponent in the center of middle court, never attempt a crosscourt shot. If it is cut off you will fall victim to a down-the-wall pass on the left side.

The drop shot is a valuable weapon in front court play. An opportune time to use

the shot (and when your opponent is probably least expecting it) is when his ceiling ball rebounds off the back wall into the middle court area. If you are aware of which side of the court he is on, try a drop shot to the opposite side. Be sure to hit the ball softly enough so that it dies shortly after bouncing off the front wall.

Often during a fast, front court rally, both players will try to kill the ball, and often will find their opponents recovering their shots. When both players are in the front court, a pass shot is always more effective. Keep an eye on your opponent's position and pass to the opposite side.

• Center Court

There is one area of the court in which most of the rallies will concentrate. This is the center court, which is roughly determined as the area immediately behind the short line and extending about 10 feet from the backwall and to within 3 feet of each side wall (Illus. 5-10).

Regardless of whether you are a front court player or a back court player, it will be to your advantage to spend as much time as possible in center court. The person who controls the center court by keeping his opponent trapped in either the front court or the back court is in control of the match. There is no better area of the court to display one's imperialistic tendencies than center court.

From center court, a player is able to attempt practically any shot with an excellent chance of success, and then is only several steps from any part of the court to retrieve his opponent's next shot.

Aggression, not passivity, is rewarded in middle court play. Once you are in midcourt, take advantage of your position by attacking the ball (but not flailing it), moving up to cut off passes and advancing quickly to front court to dispose of any missed kill shot attempts by your opponent.

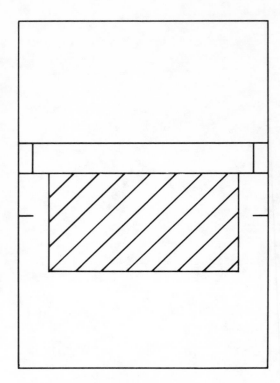

Illustration 5-10   *Center Court Area*

Illustration 5-11   *Pass your opponent with a down-the-wall shot when he is in front court.*

No matter where you are on the court, you should always move toward center court after your shot, unless you anticipate a shot in another area of the court. If you stay in front court, you are just as likely to lose the point as you are if you remain in the back court. He who hesitates is also lost in racquetball, so move after YOUR shot, not after your opponent's.

The pinch shot is an effective offensive shot from center court as long as you take into account your opponent's position. Always aim for the side wall nearest your opponent.

If you are in center court and he is to your right, shoot for the right side wall so that the ball ends up going away from him. If you were to shoot for the left side wall, the ball would follow a path directly toward your opponent.

You can use the pinch shot frequently from middle court, but avoid the reverse crosscourt pinch shot unless you can hit it with consistency.

The pass shot is as good, if not better, than the pinch shot from middle court when your opponent is in front of you. The advantage is yours in that situation because you can see where he is and aim your pass accordingly. From their advanced position, they will have difficulty reacting fast enough to cut off a pass shot.

It is usually inadvisable to attempt a kill shot when your opponent is in front of you unless it is an easy plum. A crosscourt pass or down-the-wall pass is an easier shot and more likely to be successful.

Perhaps the ideal situation is to be in front of your opponent but still in center court. Unless he tries a defensive shot, you will be in position to retrieve and score on his low percentage shots from the back court. Keep him in back court with ceiling balls or pass shots that move him from side to side so that, when you attempt a kill shot, he will have to travel the entire length of the court for a return.

For a change of pace, you may try a Z ball from center court. A good Z ball will keep your opponent in back court, and it may have him scraping his racquet against the back wall in a desperate return attempt.

• **Back Court**

This is the area roughly defined as the back ten feet in the court (Illus. 5-12).

Players who are not content to play a waiting game from the back court will usually suffer. Most mistakes occur in the back court because of the low percentage afforded offensive shots from that area.

Back court players are able to compete on a level with their faster, more aggressive opponents because of the ceiling ball, which, although it does not score many points in itself, often leads to mistakes that can be capitalized on.

One of the primary prerequisites for a good ceiling ball is the patience it takes to pass up a kill shot. If you can burden your opponent with a series of strategic ceiling

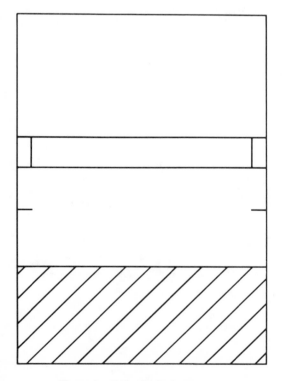

Illustration 5-12   *Back Court Area*

balls, hopefully he will make the mistake you have been avoiding but anticipating from him.

Never try a kill shot when your opponent is in front court, and only rarely when he is in center court. In the latter instance, shoot on occasion if you must to earn his respect, but only on shots with which you have full confidence.

Before attempting any shot from the back court, predetermine your chances of success. Play defensively, wait for your opponent's mistake and, when it comes, act quickly with a pass or a kill shot.

Illustration 5-13 *Try a V pass when your opponent is in front court.*

The following shot chart is designed to indicate the best shots to attempt from each area of the court and with respect to an opponent's position. The chart does not cover every possible shot from each area, merely the shots with the highest percentage of success. To determine which shots to try, find your position in the left-hand side of the chart, find your opponent's position across the top and then find the corresponding square reading across and down.

Your Opponent's Position

		Front Court	Middle Court	Back Court
Your Position—About to Hit the Ball	Front Court	Pass Do Not Shoot	Pinch Shot Drop Shot Z Ball Down-The-Wall Pass	Pinch Shot Drop Shot Front Wall-Side Wall Kill
	Middle Court	V Pass Down-The-Wall Pass Do Not Shoot	Pinch Shot Crosscourt Pass Front Wall-Side Wall Kill Ceiling Ball	Pinch Straight Kill Front Wall-Side Wall Kill Do Not Pass
	Back Court	Never Shoot Down-The-Wall Pass V Pass Crosscourt Pass Ceiling Ball	Ceiling Ball V Pass Pinch Occasionally Crosscourt Pass	Ceiling Ball Pinch Shot Straight Kill Front Wall-Side Wall Kill Do Not Pass

Illustration 5-14   *Strategy shot chart.*

PLAYING A TOURNAMENT MATCH

For the serious racquetball player, preparation for a tournament match begins long before the first serve.

There is not a right way or a wrong way to approach a match. Players have their idiosyncracies, their superstitions, their time-tested procedures, and their conditioning. I can only describe the preparations and strategy tips that have worked for me and offer them as suggestions.

• Practice

If the tournament is being played on Friday, Saturday and Sunday, I begin my pre-tournament routine the preceding Sunday after having practiced as usual for several preceeding weeks.

SUNDAY: I go through a hard workout of about four hours.

MONDAY: I play several fun games, trying to detect any flaws in my game that require extra practice. After a practice of about two hours, I run sprints for 15 minutes. I also begin to rid my diet of all sweets and concentrate on high protein foods.

TUESDAY: After a light match I run sprints and jump rope.

WEDNESDAY: I practice for about two hours, concentrating on any shots that need more work. Afterward, for light exercise, I may jog a mile, but no more sprints.

THURSDAY: I work on my equipment, making sure everything is in good shape for the tournament. I play for perhaps 30 to 45 minutes, volleying casually with someone but not keeping score.

• Preparation

Although preparations and conditioning differ for various people, I always avoid a tough match the day before a tournament. To me, a defeat would be demoralizing. Your confidence should be at a peak for your first match. My schedule is designed for me to peak during the tournament, not before.

I also avoid taking steam baths during the week so as to retain all the salt in my body for the tournament.

Some players may not want to play for a day or two before the tournament. That is something each player must decide for himself.

On the day of the match, I eat approximately two hours before the match. Diet and eating times will differ from player to player, but it is best to find a routine that works for you and then stick to it. Proper eating habits and adequate rest significantly affect a player's performance on the court.

I begin warming up about 30 minutes before the match with a short jog and light exercise. I try to be loose and relaxed when I go on the court so that my practice time can be spent working on shots. I usually spend 10 or 15 minutes warming up, but there is no time limit. Do not let your opponent or the referee rush you—take as much time as your feel is necessary.

• The Match

Assuming that I win the toss, I serve first. Since my opponent is right-handed, I start off with a garbage serve to his backhand. His judgment that the ball will come off the back wall is erroneous, and his last-second effort to retrieve the ball results in a poor return. Moving up to front court, I have no trouble putting away the plum.

Again, I try a garbage serve, and this time he rushes up for a ceiling ball return. I hit an inaccurate wallpaper ceiling ball that deflects off the side wall for an easy kill for my opponent. After only two serves, it is becoming fairly obvious that whoever makes the fewest mistakes will win.

I decided to direct my ceiling balls more toward the center of the court because, as long as he does not hit an overhead smash, a ceiling ball down the middle is just as effective as one hit along the side walls.

The first game becomes a fast, aggressive shooting game. My opponent is a good

Illustration 5-15   *Try rushing the serve and cutting off the ball before the server is set for a return.*

shooter and will try a kill from almost anywhere. I have tried to give him several enticing setups in the back court (hoping to move up and dispose of his missed kill attempts) only to find him going for winners. The percentages are against him when shooting with me in front, but so far he is succeeding.

The score is 8-3, his favor and serve. He scores four straight points because of poor service returns. From the crowd, I hear a friend suggest that I call time-out. While you should not usually pay much attention to what is said or yelled from the crowd,

sometimes an observer can detect something that you had not noticed.

I take the time-out in an attempt to regain my concentration. After resuming play and regaining the serve, I notice that my opponent is beginning to hit the ball harder and with less control as the game progresses.

His fast pace and hard rallies have earned him 13 points to my 8. Perceiving my chances of winning to be slim, I begin to feed him a steady diet of ceiling balls. I know I am in good shape and, if nothing else this game, I will find out if he is.

He wins his two points for the game, but the rallies last ten minutes. I have improved my chances in the last two games by forcing him to expend a maximum amount of energy in the first.

During the two minute rest period between games I change my shirt and socks so that I will feel as fresh as possible the next game.

I resume my ceiling ball barrage as the second game begins in an effort to tire my opponent even further. Not only do I take an 8-0 lead, but I notice my opponent is becoming worried about wearing himself out. He is at a distinct disadvantage now, because he should be worrying about the game and not about his approaching state of exhaustion.

Most of my points have been scored with garbage serves to the corner. When a player begins to tire, he stops attacking the ball and allows it to come to him. My hours of practice are paying off. My serves are going to the corner and staying in the corner.

My opponent stops hitting ceiling ball returns because he wants to avoid another long rally. With a large lead and the game seemingly in hand, I stop shooting altogether and prolong my efforts to tire my opponent. I opt for pass shots, sending him on a tour of the court. I integrate my attack with additional ceiling balls and an occasional Z ball if he comes to front court.

Realizing that he will get a five minute

rest period before the third game, I run him relentlessly in hopes that those two minutes will not be enough for him to recover. My strategy works so well that when the score reaches 12-5, he has already used his allotted time-outs. He throws away the last three points, thereby avoiding the unnecessary loss of further energy.

Despite his fatigue, he is able to find his second wind and enter the third game with a revitalized attitude after the five minute rest period. He has wisely brought along a friend and counselor who helps him straighten out his thoughts and regain his composure. From his detached position in the stands, his friend can detect some of his mistakes and offer suggestions on different strategy.

In the third game my opponent switches to a front court attack, but I score several straight points because he is not quick enough to react to the hard drives I hit right at him.

On my garbage serves, he begins to move up and hit them before they reach the back wall, so I switch to a lob serve.

The best way to counteract his new front court tactics is with the use of pass shots. Several times I am about to try a kill shot from the front court and I notice he is moving up, so I decide at the last second to hit a down-the-wall pass instead.

Considering his weakened physical condition, he puts up a good fight in the third game, but with a combination of ceiling balls, passes, a few kill shots, and patience, I win the game and the match. By out-thinking my opponent, I was able to defeat an excellent shooter.

Even though I lost the first game, I all but guaranteed victory in the third game by exhausting my opponent in the second game. It was not just a good serve or a good ceiling ball that won the match. Thoughtful strategy and the composure needed to carry it out were just as important.

STRATEGY TIPS

- Take a minute to introduce yourself to your opponent(s). Try to evaluate their confidence and mental attitude.
- Check out the court for any peculiarities (i.e., irregular walls, protruding door frames, cracks in panels, etc.) that can affect the bounce of the ball.
- Bring additional equipment in case of breakage or damage.
- Watch your opponents carefully as they warm-up.
- Check the audience to see if you have any possible "allies" that might offer constructive criticism between the games.

- Evaluate the referee as the game progresses. Determine if he/she is unprejudiced and professional, nit-picky, half blind or downright nuts. Use this information to your advantage. Referee calls can affect the outcome of a close game.
- Remember to forget the crowds and concentrate on formulating and executing your strategy as the game progresses.

Illustration 5-6 *Randy cuts a ball off in center court and executes a drop shot while his opponent is still in back center court. Again, strategy pays off.*

Illustration 6-1   *This is one of the first metal racquets ever made, called the "Dayton."*
I used to play with this old racquet when I was 15 years old. It was made in 1969 and had steel strings.

chapter 6

ALL ABOUT RACQUETBALL

I have decided to devote this chapter to several general areas of the sport of racquetball. These areas include hinders, how to use positioning to your advantage, and a section on certain rules relating to the little discussed area of racquetball play for the beginner. Also included are discussions on footwork, concentration and conditioning.

For more detail, please refer to the rules section in Chapter Eight. Last and probably most important, is a section on the unwritten rules of racquetball. This covers courtesy, respect for the game, and respect for your opponent.

HINDERS AND ADVANCED STRATEGY

If there is a flaw in the game of racquetball, it must be the often controversial gray area known as "hinders."

The rule is simple enough: An opponent must be given a clear and unobstructed path to the ball. It is the interpretation and execution of the rule that causes problems. (Rule 11.C).

A player's swing cannot be obstructed in any way. He must be given a clear and unblocked shot. After a player hits the ball, he must give his opponent a fair chance to see or return the ball, otherwise an "avoidable hinder" may be called.

Any obstruction of the swing or access to the ball, whether on purpose or by accident, can be ruled an avoidable hinder. If the call is against the server, there is a sideout. Conversely, a point to the server

is awarded if the receiver is faced with an avoidable hinder.

It is strictly a judgment call, and it puts a tremendous burden on the referee, especially during a doubles match.

Another type of hinder is the screen ball, which occurs when an obstruction of view results from the ball passing too close to a player. It is advisable to avoid hinder calls, but, in so doing, do not give your opponent so much room that you put yourself in a disadvantageous court position.

Illustration 6-2 *Playing too close to your opponent could result in being struck with a racquet.*

There are ways to use the hinder rules to your advantage, although beginning players would be better off learning the game before attempting to play these techniques.

Illustration 6-3 *By positioning one's self in this situation, your opponent's shots are limited.*

Hinder strategy is not only difficult to apply, but it can cause a player to be hit with the ball or his opponent's racquet (Illus. 6-2).

With experience a player will be able to intimidate an opponent just short of being called for a hinder or being accused of unsportsmanlike conduct.

One of the best ways to put your opponent at a disadvantage is by limiting his choice of shots. For instance, if your opponent is about to hit a forehand from near the right side wall in middle or back court, you can position yourself so as to limit him to a ceiling ball or a down-the-wall shot. If you are to the front and left of him, he cannot go for a crosscourt pass.

Most players will attempt only those shots for which they have an unobstructed path. The most experienced player may detect your strategy and attempt to counteract it by going for the crosscourt pass, even though you are in the way. Most players are persuaded to move after absorbing several hard shots in the back.

It may be possible to disturb your opponent's concentration during a long ceiling ball rally by moving fairly close to him while he is hitting the ball. Do not get so close that the referee calls a hinder or you get hit by the racquet, resulting in a "waffle face". Just let him know you are there (anything to take his mind off hitting the ball).

When you are making a shot, do not restrict your follow-through simply because your opponent is crowding. If you will make him respect your hitting area, you will always have plenty of room in which to execute your stroke.

OVERVIEW OF THE RULES

During play, a normal match consists of two out of three games with the first two being played to 15. If a tie breaker is required, it is played to 11. It is not necessary to win by two points.

To serve, you stand inside the service zone, (standing on a line is acceptable) drop the ball and then hit it on the first bounce so that it strikes the front wall first. On the rebound, the ball should hit the floor behind the short line either with or without touching one of the sidewalls. At this point, the opponent starts the rally by returning the serve. You then have two chances to hit a good serve. Examples of bad serves are as follows: a long serve (the ball hits the back wall before the floor); a short serve (when a served ball hits the front wall and on the rebound does not hit past the short line); or a three-wall serve. A ceiling serve, first foot fault, or an out-court serve are also examples of bad serves which allow the server another attempt at a successful serve. Examples of an immediate sideout serve or "out serve" are when a server takes longer than ten seconds to serve, a missed or fake serve, a ball that when served strikes the server, or their racquet, or a crotch serve. Also when the server hits a wall other than the front wall first (i.e., a side wall), on out-of-order serve (doubles), or when the server moves out of the service area before the ball passes the short line.

The receiver must stand behind the receiving line and cannot enter into the safety zone until the ball bounces past the short-line or past the receiving line on the fly. The receiver must return a good serve or lose a point. To return the ball, you must hit the serve before it strikes the floor twice. You must return the ball to the front wall, being sure not to hit the floor first. Any combination of walls is fine, as long as the ball hits the front wall before the floor. This initiates the rally, with each volley played in the same manner as described above. The lines on the floor are of no significance during a rally, as you only need to be concerned with them during the service.

During a rally, the racquet strings must be used to hit the ball. Anything else results in a sideout. If you miss a ball during a rally, you may repeat your attempt until the ball hits the floor a second time. Any ball that hits the front wall and then caroms out of the court shall be declared dead and the serve replayed. If you hit a ball out of the court before striking the front wall, you lose the rally. A broken ball during the rally will result in a replay of that point.

There are two types of hinders: "dead ball" hinders and "avoidable" hinders. The first results in the point being replayed. Examples of "dead ball hinders" are when a ball hits a predetermined court hinder, hitting an opponent on the fly as the ball is traveling toward the front wall, or body contact that interferes with seeing or returning the ball, a screen ball and a safety/holdup. Avoidable hinders result in an "out" or a point depending upon whether the offender was serving or receiving. Common examples are failure to move and allow an opponent a clear shot, pushing, blocking, and moving into a ball such that you prevent any clear shot toward the front wall. Hinders are usually judgement calls and require a certain amount of understanding from both players.

A few racquetball words you need to be familiar with are the skipshot, short and long serve, crotch ball and 3-wall serve. A "skip" ball usually makes a distinct sound when it hits the floor. Remember the "skip" ball is a bad shot that hits the floor before the front wall. A short serve is one that does not clear the short line, while a long serve hits the backwall before striking the floor. Both of these serves are "bad" serves. When one occurs during a serve, simply say "short" or "long" so that your opponent can hear you. A crotch ball is when the ball hits a juncture of two playing surfaces simultaneously. A crotch ball on the front wall would be considered a "skip" ball while a crotch ball that occurs while serving to a side wall would probably result in an "ace." A 3-wall serve is always a bad serve. But a serve that strikes the front wall, then a side wall and hits the floor and then another side wall is considered a good serve.

FOOTWORK

Of all the different aspects of racquetball and, for that matter, sports in general, footwork is probably the most underrated and the most taken for granted. As heat is essential to cooking, so is footwork to good racquetball.

It would be simple if the ball would cooperate by coming to you after your opponent's every shot. If that were possible, this section could have been omitted and we could have gone on to discuss the more exciting elements of the game, such as strategy and the process of outsmarting your opponent. But as it is the nature of the game to hit the ball away from your opponent, rather than to him, the necessity of learning proper footwork becomes obvious.

Footwork is unique in the sense that it is the only ingredient of proper shot-making that will, by necessity, change every time you hit the ball. It has been, and will be, stressed throughout this book that consistency in the swing is essential. Of course, the angle of the shot, its height, where you plan to hit it, etc., will all have their influence on your swing, but the fundamentals of the shot remain the same. Getting to the ball via footwork is another matter.

It is possible that the placement of your feet may never be the same for any two shots during a match. The distance to be covered to reach a shot, the time you have to get there, the location of your opponent, and the type of shot you plan to hit all combine to force a change in the placement of feet for each shot. It is therefore a fundamental requirement of the game to master the art of footwork.

One of the more important things to

Illustration 6-4 *Remember, stay on your toes.*

remember about footwork is to keep the knees bent. When a person is standing straight-legged, the first thing he does before beginning to run is an involuntary and unconscious bending of the knees. Make sure they are slightly bent and remain slightly bent throughout the point to improve your reaction time..

Ordinarily, the saying "stay on your toes" is an encouragement to be alert. In the case of footwork, however, it is to be taken in its most literal sense. Overall quickness is immeasurably increased and reaction time immeasurably decreased by staying posed on your toes. If you have trouble staying up for a shot once you have arrived in the general area of the ball, try bouncing lightly on your toes. It will facilitate bringing your feet into proper position to swing the racquet.

The feet must be kept apart, but not too far apart. With your feet close together, you may trip if you suddenly turn for a quick pass. By the same token, the feet can be placed too far apart, resulting in slow and awkward movement. The proper stance depends on the individual. Usually, the feet should be about a shoulder width apart while standing poised in anticipation of the next shot. When more than one or two quick steps are needed in moving for a shot, the first step should be taken with the foot furthest from your destination (i.e., move the left foot first to go right, the back foot first to go forward, etc.). By doing so, you will have avoided any unnecessary steps that could have caused you to miss, rather than reach, the ball.

Movement is vitally important to racquetball. This sport has been known as a long-distance sprint. During play, try to develop a smooth, flowing technique. Always move to center court after hitting the ball, trying to anticipate your opponent's next shot.

When a player becomes fatigued, footwork is often the first part of his game to suffer. It is very difficult to hit a ceiling ball

Illustration 6-5 *Larry shows his expert diving form.*

while stretching over your shoulder and running after the ball. This shot can be made more easily by moving quickly and efficiently to outrace the ball, then moving into proper position to step into the ball for a balanced swing. Inadequate "hustle" and improper footwork are often the downfall of an exhausted or lazy player.

DIVING

Diving is a technique of last resort being used by many players today. It is dangerous in the sense that a player is in poor position for a return if he does not hit a winner. More importantly, it can also be physically dangerous.

Diving for the ball is sometimes the only possible way to make a return, but it should not be attempted until it can be performed safely (Illus. 6-5).

If you are an avid player who wants to learn all the aspects of the game, you should know the correct technique.

It is recommended that you land on your chest or shoulder. If you occasionally land on your knees, wear knee pads to minimize the possiblity of injury.

There are right times to dive and wrong times to dive. Unless you are particularly adept, dive only when you cannot reach the ball any other way. When the score is 2-2 or 14-2 it is unwise to dive. When the score is 14-14, an experienced player may want to consider diving.

However, if you are a player who desires fun and wants to minimize destruction of your body, then by all means do not dive. You will still reap plenty of the other benefits racquetball has to offer.

CONCENTRATION

Once a racquetball player has trained his mind and his body to physically respond in the form of a devastating forehand, a well-placed backhand or an irretrievable serve, it is time to work on the mental part of the game. To become a successful player, that intangible mental sharpness, otherwise known as concentration, must be attained and maintained.

Unfortunately, there are not many drills a player can perform or diagrams he can draw to improve his ability to concentrate. Some people are innately better at concentrating than others, so that it is not impossible for a player of lesser physicial strength and skill to defeat a superior opponent. Lapses in concentration can be as destructive as a poorly devised strategy or lack of conditioning.

Concentration is not easily defined, nor easily mastered. One thing, however, is certain, and that is that concentration should be involved in each aspect of your game. For instance, when you are hitting a ceiling ball a number of things should be going through your mind: thinking about the correct stroke and follow-through, where to go after hitting the ceiling ball, where your opponent may hit his next shot, or how hard to hit your shot. All these possibilites deserve your concentration.

Illustration 6-6 *Concentration and watching the ball are essential for playing well.*

ponents are my fundamentals. I know my limits, my shots, and I know I will hustle. Each will change very little from match to match, so that I can concentrate my attention on the variable components—my strategy and my opponent. I therefore adjust to each situation by changing my strategy, if necessary, but not my fundamentals. I look at my opponent and size him up in order to decide what type of strategy I should use.

There is little to compare with the pleasure derived from outsmarting your opponent. If he is in the back court and, expecting a short shot of some kind, comes rushing forward, only to be beaten with a passing shot to the back court, you will have reaped the benefits of concentration. Without it, you might not have known where he was and where he was going.

Without concentration, your performance is limited. With it, your shots become sharper, your movement has a definite pupose and your confidence is heightened. For instance, a player's instinct tells him to chase the ball the moment it comes off the wall. If he does, he may find that he has run all over the court, only to discover that the ball ended up at the point where he began running. Energy and aggravation can be spared by concentrating, thinking, and anticipating where the ball will end up.

There are some subtle and not-so-subtle methods players have used to maintain concentration. Some players need only begin the game thinking about what they should do. Others need constant reminders. It is not uncommon to hear someone in the stands send down a vocal reminder to concentrate. It may even be necessary to write "concentrate" on your hand. Any device or scheme to help you concentrate is well worth the effort.

Unfortunately, some players will never be able to concentrate, even if the word were

It is nearly impossible to concentrate every minute of every match because of the tendency for the mind to wander. Yet, the closer a player can come to 100 percent concentration, the more complete and well-rounded his game will be. If he is thinking about his last mistake while attempting a kill on the next point, chances are he will miss the shot. It is fine to ponder a missed shot, but only until the next point begins.

It is important that a beginning player concentrate on the techniques of hitting the various shots, footwork, or any other fundamental. Eventually, the shots and the footwork will become habit, making it possible to concentrate on other aspects of the match such as where to hit the ball, where to move, or your opponent's strategy.

In each match there are fixed components and variable components. The fixed com-

stenciled in foot-high letters on the front wall. If you realize the value of concentration you will be the better player for having done so.

PHYSICAL CONDITION

It is likely that in a match between two players of virtually equal ability, the player who is in better physical condition will win. As suggested in the section entitled "Playing a Tournament Match," it is even possible to defeat a superior opponent by testing his stamina.

Poor conditioning is every bit as much of a liability as a poor backhand, forehand or serve. Tired players make for tired shots. If you are out of shape and exhausted, you are sapped of your ability to get full use out of the skills you have acquired.

The amount of conditioning necessary is dependent on a player's level of competition. There are those who play only once or twice a week, simply for the purpose of having a good time and regular exercise. The more serious player who competes three to five times a week probably will work himself into adequate physical condition by the act of playing.

For the player who enters tournaments, on-the-court activity is not sufficient. It should be supplemented by strenuous exercise and conditioning. If you are ever called upon to play three grueling matches of two to three games each in one day, you will understand why.

Popular conditioning exercises include jogging, sprints, jumping rope, swimming, lifting weights, pushups, pullups, and situps. They are not intended to make a player muscle-bound, but only to prepare him for a rigorous tournament match.

Nothing is better than running for building up the legs and stamina. Before a practice match I will do 350 to 450 jump ropes and, after one to three hours of playing, finish my workout by doing either

sprints or long-distance running. A lot of the boredom of exercising can be eliminated by variety.

My sprints consist of about 15 minutes of hard running for short distances, which is enough to completely wear me out. Every other day or so, I will run two to four miles, which, along with jumping rope and sprints, builds up my legs and increases my stamina.

I exercise my upper body in the mornings by doing situps and pushups. It is relatively easy to decide how many of each to do. When you cannot do any more, you have done enough. Only by pushing yourself and making the muscles really work will you get much benefit out of exercise.

The serious tournament player must not only reach a certain level of conditioning, but he also has to maintain it or, better yet, continue to improve it. It is unrealistic to enter a tournament in poor shape and expect to win many matches. It is also unrealistic to expect to get in shape in a short period of time. Peak physical condition is the end product of several months of work.

Work out a conditioning schedule for yourself and do your best to stick with it. The extra stamina and the muscles you develop will pay off on the court.

UNWRITTEN RULES

It is late in the third game of a tense, closely contested tournament match. Each succeeding point is of crucial importance to the match. You are in middle court and your opponent, positioned in front court, tries a drop shot. Your only chance for a return is a dive. You lunge and, as far as the referee and your opponent can tell, you reach the ball just before its second bounce and hit a winner to advance one point closer to victory.

The trouble is that you and you alone realize the ball bounced twice before you were able to hit it. Do you accept the referee's decision in your favor, or do you speak up and forfeit the point by informing him of the second bounce? This is the essence of sportsmanship—the unwritten rules of racquetball.

The rules state that players must abide by the referee's decision, so you are within the rules when you accept a favorable decision that you know to be in error. The only rule you are breaking is the unwritten rule that urges players to call points against themselves out of respect for the game, their opponents and, ultimately, themselves.

If, during a pickup game, there is a disagreement between players on a call, the point should be replayed. Some calls are extremely difficult to make, such as a crotch ball (one that hits the floor and front wall simultaneously) or a skip ball (one that skips along the floor just before hitting the front wall). It is senseless to waste time arguing over a call that is easily perceived differently by the players. Just replay the point.

Being hit with the ball or a racquet should be understood as part of the game. Nevertheless, it is possible to avoid most accidents and injuries if the player hitting the ball uses discretion and sportsmanship. If your opponent is crowding you, there are better ways of letting him know he is too close than hitting him with the racquet. It is an unwritten rule that a player stop his swing and call a safety hinder if he is sure the ball will hit his opponent. After one or two such hinders, he will realize that he is in the way. Most players appreciate a safety hinder as an alternative to being hit with the ball.

Whenever the ball leaves the court, either player, upon request, should be allowed to examine the ball to make sure it is playable. It is nothing more than simple courtesy. It is a requirement in tournament matches to check the ball after it hits a player. And, to insure that a broken ball is not put into play, it should be checked after it makes an unusual sound or bounce during play.

Illustration 6-7 *Your wrist thong can be attached two different ways. See chapter one for details.*

Illustration 6-8 *Cutthroat can be a popular game. See chapter seven for details.*

Illustration 6-9 *Thanking your opponent for a good game is simple courtesy.*

It is a violation of the unwritten rules to disturb your opponent's concentation by making any loud or unnecessary noises. Keep your composure on the court. Do not argue with your opponent. If he wants to offer assistance, it is his prerogative.

If you wish to raise a point of contention during the match, do so calmly with the referee. Bad calls inevitably are made; they are part of the game. They usually even out in the long run, and they rarely affect the outcome of a match.

There is a fine line between a skip and a kill, and it can only be detected accurately by watching and listening. Although a skipping sound usually indicates a skip, the same sound can be produced by hitting the side wall in front court. In such an instance, only visual detection is possible. On the other hand, a skip can occur without the skipping sound. As difficult as skips are to detect at times, it is pointless to argue back and forth. Replay the point.

The unwritten rules of racquetball basically call for honesty, mature behavior, and respect for the game and for other players. As corny as it may sound, honesty does breed honesty. If you call a point against yourself, your opponent can hardly help but do the same when the opportunity presents itself.

Illustration 7-1 *A down-the-wall pass is an excellent choice in a doubles match.*

chapter 7

DOUBLES

Doubles is a complex game that requires even more patience than singles. With four players on the court, any kill shot has to be hit almost perfectly to be a winner. It often becomes very tempting during long ceiling ball rallies to try a kill, so it is necessary to exercise patience and wait until you are sure of hitting a winner. The pinch shot is therefore often used with success as a kill in doubles.

POSITIONING FOR DOUBLES

Crowding is a problem inherent in the game of doubles. The better the two teammates stay away from each other, the better their court coverage will be. There are four basic formations for doubles court coverage: side by side, I-formation, center exchange and limited position technique.

• Side by Side

The side by side method is probably the most widely used today. Each player is responsible for coverage of an area to either side of an imaginary line drawn down the middle of the court. The line need not be drawn exactly down the middle, and it is possible and sometimes necessary to step over into a teammate's territory.

Assuming both players are right-handed, the player with the better backhand should be on the left side. He can take the shots down the middle, as well as shots to his backhand. His teammate, the one with the weaker backhand, can therefore concentrate on shots to his forehand (Illus. 7-2).

Illustration 7-2 *Side by side court coverage for doubles.*

If both players are left-handed, the one with the best backhand should be on the side, for similar reasons. If one player is right-handed and one is left-handed, the right-hander should be on the right side and the left-hander should be on the left. The player with the better backhand can take the shots down the middle.

• I-Formation

The I-formation with players positioned front and back is usually not highly effective, and, as such, is seldom used. It requires that one extremely quick player take the front court and that a good shooter and ceiling ball player take the back court. In most cases, it is too much work for the back court player and too much responsiblity for the front court player.

• Center Court Exchange

The center court exchange method is a bit more complicated, but it has its advantages if used correctly. The two partners, who should both be quick and aggressive, should decide which side of the court each

Illustration 7-3   *Center Exchange Doubles Method.*

will cover, as with the side by side method.

In addition, when one player is hitting the ball, his teammate will always move into the center of the middle court area. If the middle court partner is forced into back court for a return, his teammate automatically takes his right place at midcourt. (Illus. 7-3).

With this formation, a player always knows where his teammate is when he hits the ball. And, because their teammate is located in the approximate center of the court, a player can try a crosscourt pass or down-the-wall pass, knowing that the ball will not hit their partner before or after coming off the front wall.

• Limited Position

If one player is far better than his teammate, the limited position technique is the most effective. The principles of the half and half method are used, except that the imaginary line is moved farther to one side to give the better player more coverage responsibility (Illus. 7-4).

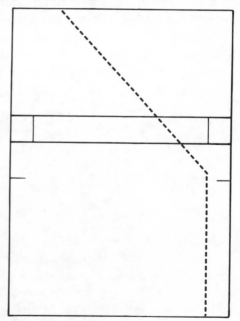

Illustration 7-4   *Limited Position Strategy For Doubles.*

SERVICE

The service is probably tougher in doubles than in singles. This is because your

Illustration 7-5 *Proper serving position for doubles.*

opponents are already closer to the point of contact on the initial service return. First decide which of the two opponents are the weakest and which service would be most effective. The same principles for singles apply in doubles as well. Try to force your opponents to return the ball from the back corners. If the team has both a right-handed player and a lefty, then the backhands will end up in the middle court. Try serving crosscourt serves that end up about waist high in the back middle court.

One problem is serving hard drives or "Z" serves to the back corner of your partner's side of the court. The tendency is for your opponent to move up, cutting the ball off and drilling your partner in the back with the ball. This will definitely result in a lower performance from your partner. I would recommend changing serves to a garbage or lob serve. This would give your opponent time to set up.

I have found the following service strategy to be effective. Since both of you are placed in the center court while serving, why not take advantage of the situation. Try serving the ball such that you give your opponent a difficult kill shot attempt from 35 feet. A temptation like this is difficult for most players to pass up. Hopefully, they will try this kill leaving the ball up perhaps 6 inches, giving you the opportunity for a third shot rekill. If you are serving from the left side of the service zone to the left back wall, there are only several return of serve shots for you to anticipate. If you move slightly to the left to cover a down-the-line pass and your partner stays up front to cover for the pinch and crosscourt pass, most of your opponents' options are covered. If a pass or a ceiling is hit successfully, you will probably have to retrieve it from the back wall. But, the main point is that this strategy makes

Illustration 7-6 *A serve to the middle of the backcourt can be a good choice if your opponents' backhands are to the center of the court.*

Illustration 7-7 *Setting up after service is important. Notice how Randy is facing the side wall anticipating the return. Watch your opponent setup for the return, but don't watch while they hit it.*

doubles fun to play. The serve is planned out, you are anticipating the return while at the same time setting up in position to cover all available options. This is playing strategic racquetball.

• Service Movement

The center court is the only place to be in doubles. After service, you must very quickly move out of the box a couple of steps—moving to the side of the court, ready for a return. If you serve a hard serve, you must react quickly and be setup for a fast return. One should practically sprint out of the service box and setup. If you have trouble setting up for the next shot quickly, stick with slower serves like the lobs or garbage serves. After serving, try to move only two or three steps out of the box and toward the side of the court where the ball is served. The key is to maintain center court, but focus your team slightly to the side of the court where the play is concentrated. This allows you to cut off down-the-wall passes.

• Doubles Rally

The number one consideration in doubles is to maintain center court. By maintaining center court and cutting off the ball from chest high or lower, a team can be devastating. Personally, I recommend the combination of the side by side doubles and center exchange doubles method. This allows for both the players to be in center court when the opponents are in back court, but also gives you the location of your opponent when you retrieve shots in the front or back court. Played at its optimum, doubles is a very aggressive game, even more so than singles.

Beginners, do not fret. There is plenty of room for you on the doubles court. *The very first action you take in a doubles match is to put on your eyeguards.* They may be uncomfortable at first, but they are a necessity, so get used to them. Now, let us get on to playing the match safely.

You need to recognize that your game tempo is not as fast or accurate as other players. That is not a problem, because racquetball has a strategy for everyone. Being slower on the court, learn to hit shots that fit your game style. During service, try a lob or garbage serve. Occasionally try medium speed Z serves. The reason for these serves is to give you time to set up, before the ball is blasted back at you. Try maintaining a position further back into the center court zone. This gives you a larger picture of the court and more time to react. During the rally, if you are not set up for a high percentage kill shot, then look for a ceiling ball or pass shot. Keep your opponents moving out of center court to the back corners with your nicely-placed, ceiling shots. Hopefully, if they try a kill shot from 37 feet, you will anticipate this opportunity by moving up (your opponent goes to center court) and catching the ball for a rekill. In doubles, patience is important as one mistake will cause you to lose a point and could move the momentum to the other team's advantage.

• Service Return

Attention to the service return in doubles is even more important than singles. The reason is because there are two players in center court rather than one. Unless you are able to bottomboard kill shots, you should hit a ceiling ball or pass shot as a defensive move to put your opponents in back court with your team in center court. I prefer the best of both worlds and hit a lot of down-the-line, pass-kill shots. If I miss this kill, the pass will hopefully send my opponent scurrying to the back court while I do my Texas two-step right around him to center court.

The main point to remember is that your opponents are in center court where you are supposed to be. Be patient and try not to give away points. Make your opponents earn them.

American Amateur Racquetball Association (AARA)
815 N. Weber, Suite 101
Colorado Springs, CO 80903
(Please write for membership information.)

1982-84 AARA OFFICIAL RULE BOOK
(Note: Rules are continually revised. For any modifications after 2-1-87, contact the AARA for rule updates.)

1—THE GAME

A. TYPES OF GAMES

Racquetball may be played by two, three, or four players. When played by two it is called "singles", when played by three, "cutthroat", and when played by four, "doubles".

B. DESCRIPTION

Racquetball is a competitive game in which each player uses a racquet to serve and return the ball.

C. OBJECTIVE

The objective is to win each rally by serving or returning the ball so the opponent is unable to keep the ball in play. A rally is over when a side makes an error, or is unable to return the ball before it touches the floor twice, or if a hinder is called.

D. POINTS AND OUTS

Points are scored only by the (server/serving team) when it serves an ace or wins a rally. When the serving side loses a rally, it loses the serve. Losing the serve is called an "out" in singles, and a "handout", or "sideout" in doubles.

E. GAME

A game is won by the side first scoring 15 points. The third game, referred to as the tiebreaker, is played to 11. It is necessary to win only by one point.

F. MATCH

A match is won by the first side winning two games. The first two games of a match are played to 15 points. In the event each side wins one game, the match shall be decided by an 11-point tiebreaker.

G. DOUBLES TEAM

A doubles team shall consist of two players that meet either/or the age requirements or player classification requirements to participate in a particular division of play. A team must be classified by the ability level (or player classification) of the higher ranked player on the team.

A change in playing partners may not be made after the final draw has been made and posted. Under no circumstances can a partner change be made during the course of a tournament without the consent of the Tournament Director.

H. CONSOLATION MATCHES

1) Consolation matches may be waived at the discretion of the Tournament Director, but this waiver must be in writing on the tournament application.
2) Since each entrant shall be entitled to participate in a minimum of two matches, losers of their first match shall have the opportunity to compete in a consolation bracket of their own division. In draws of less than seven players, a round robin format may be offered.
3) Preliminary consolation matches will be two of three games to 11 points. Semifinals and finals matches will follow the regular scoring format.

2—COURTS AND EQUIPMENT

A. COURTS

The specifications for the standard four wall racquetball court are:

1) **Dimension.** The dimensions shall be 20 feet wide, 20 feet high, and 40 feet long, with a back wall at least 12 feet high. All surfaces within the court shall be deemed "in play" with the exception of any gallery openings or surfaces designated as "court hinders."

2) **Lines and Zones.** Racquetball courts shall be divided and marked with 1½ inch wide lines as follows:

   a) **Short Line.** The back edge of the short line is midway between (20 ft.) and parallel to, the front and back walls, thus dividing the court into equal front and back courts.

   b) **Service Line.** The front edge of the service line is five feet in front of the back edge of the short line.

   c) **Service Zone.** The service zone is the area between the outer edges of the short line and service line.

   d) **Service Boxes.** The services boxes are located at each end of the service zone and are designated by lines parallel with each side wall. The inside edge of the lines are 18 inches from the side walls.

   e) **Receiving Line.** A broken line parallel to the short line. The back edge of the receiving line will be five feet from the back edge of the short line. The receiving line will begin with a line 21 inches long that extends from each side wall: the two lines will be connected by an alternate series of six-inch spaces and six-inch lines (17 six-inch spaces and 16 six-inch lines).

   f) **Safety Zone.** The five-foot area bounded by the short line and the receiving line. The zone is observed only during the serve. The effect of entering the zone prematurely is: 1) if the receiver, or partner in doubles, commits the infraction, it results in a point; 2) if the server, or partner, commits the infraction, it results in the loss of serve. (see Rule 8.A. and 7.1.)

B. BALL SPECIFICATIONS

1) The standard racquetball shall be 2¼" in diameter; weigh approximately 1.4 ounces, and

at a temperature of 70-74°F., with a 100 inch drop, rebound to 68-72 inches and have a hardness of 55-60 inches durometer.

2) Any ball which carries the endorsement of approval from the AARA is an official ball. Only AARA approved balls may be used in AARA sanctioned tournaments.

C. BALL SELECTION

1) A ball shall be selected by the referee for use in each match. During the match, the referee either at his discretion, or at the request of a player or team, may replace the game ball. Balls that are not round or which bounce erratically shall not be used.

2) In tournament play, the referee and the players shall agree to an alternate ball, so that in the event of breakage, the second ball can be put into play immediately.

D. RACQUET SPECIFICATIONS (Effective 9/1/86)

1) **Dimensions.** The racquet, including bumper guard and all solid parts of the handle, may not exceed 21 inches in length.

2) The racquet frame may be of any material judged to be safe.

3) The regulation racquet frame must include a thong that must be securely attached to the player's wrist.

4) The string of the racquet should be gut, monofilament, nylon, graphite, plastic, metal, or a combination thereof, providing strings do not mark or deface the ball.

E. UNIFORM

1) The uniform and shoes may be of any color but must have soles which do not mark or damage the court floor. The shirt may contain any insignia or writing considered in good taste by the Tournament Director. Players are required to wear shirts. Extremely loose fitting or otherwise distracting garments are not permissable.

2) Eye protection is required for any participant under the age of 19 in all AARA sanctioned tournaments. **NOTE:** For failing to wear eye protection or wear the guards properly over the eyes, the AARA recommends: Upon notice of the first violation, the referee may issue a technical and require the player to take a timeout to secure eye protection. Second notice of an infraction in the same match may result in a forfeit. The eyeguards may not be altered; if the eyeguards are designed to have lenses, the lenses must be in place. (Effective 9/1/86).

3—OFFICIATING AND PLAY REGULATIONS

RULE 1. TOURNAMENTS

Rule 1. A. Tournament Management

All tournaments shall be managed by a committee or Tournament Director who shall designate the officials.

Rule 1. B. Officials

The official shall be a referee designated by the Tournament Director or the floor manager or one agreed to by both participants (teams in doubles). Officials may also include, at the discretion of the tournament director, a scorekeeper and two line judges.

Rule 1. C. Removal of Referee

A referee may be removed upon the agreement of all participants (teams in doubles) or at the discretion of the tournament director or rules officials. In the event that a referee's removal is requested by one player or team and not agreed to by the other, the Tournament Director or officials may accept or reject the request. The Tournament Director or rules official may observe a match in progress to determine what, if any, action is to be taken.

Rule 1. D. Rule Briefing

Before all tournaments, all officials and players shall be briefed on rules and on court hinders, regulations, and modifications the Tournament Director wishes to impose. This briefing should be reduced to writing. The current AARA rules will apply and be made available. Any modifications the Tournament Director wishes to impose must be stated on the entry form and in writing and be available to all players at registration.

Rule 1. E. Referees

1) **Pre-match duties.** Before each match begins, it shall be the duty of the referee to:

   a) Check on adequacy of preparation of court with respect to cleanliness, lighting, and temperature.

   b) Check on availability and suitability of materials—to include balls, towels, scorecards, pencils, and time-piece—necessary for the match.

   c) Go on court to instruct players.

   d) Point out court hinders and note any local regulations.

   e) Inspect equipment and toss coin.

   f) Check line judges and scorekeeper and ask for reserve game ball upon assuming officiating position.

   g) Review any rule modifications in effect for this particular tournament.

2) **Decisions.** During the match, the referee shall make all decisions with regard to the rules. Where line judges are used, the referee shall announce all final judgments. If both players in singles and three out of four in a doubles match disagree with a judgment call made by the referee, the referee is overruled. The referee shall have jurisdiction over the spectators as well as players while the match is in progress.

3) **Protests.** Any decision not involving the judgment of the referee may, on protest, be decided by the Tournament Director or designated official.

4) **Forfeitures.** A match may be forfeited by the referee when:
   a) Any player refuses to abide by the referee's decision, or engages in unsportsmanlike conduct.
   b) Any player or team who fails to report to play 10 minutes after the match has been scheduled to play. (The Tournament Director may permit a longer delay if circumstances warrant such a decision.)
5) **Defaults.** A player or team may be forfeited by the Tournament Director or official for failure to comply with the tournament or host facility's rules while on the premises, for failure to referee, for improper conduct on the premises between matches, or for abuse of hospitality, locker room, or other rules and procedures.
6) **Other Rulings.** The referee may rule on all matters not covered in the AARA Official Rules. However, the referee may be overruled by the Tournament Director.

Rule 1. F. Line Judges
1) Two line judges are recommended for all matches from the semifinals on up, subject to availability and the discretion of the tournament officials. The line judges shall be selected by the officials and situated as designated by the officials. If any player objects to the selection of a line judge before the match begins, all reasonable effort shall be made to find a replacement acceptable to the officials and players. If a player or team objects to a line judge after the match begins, replacement shall be under the discretion of the referee and officials.
2) Line judges are designated in order to help decide appealed rulings. Two line judges will be designated by the referee and shall, at the referee's signal, either agree or disagree with the referee's ruling. The signal by a line judge to show agreement with the referee is "thumbs up". The signal to show disagreement is "thumbs down." The signal for no opinion is "open palms down".

If both line judges signal no opinion, the referee's call stands. If both line judges disagree with the referee, the referee must reverse the ruling. If one line judge agrees and one disagrees or has no opinion, the referee's call shall stand. If one line judge disagrees and one has no opinion, the rally or serve shall be replayed. Any replays will result in two serves with the exception of appeals on the second serve itself.

Rule 1. G. Appeals
In any match using line judges, a player or team may appeal only the following calls or non-calls by the referee: killshots and skip balls; fault serves; out serves; double-bounce pickups; receiving line violations; rule interpretations.

The appeal must be directed to the referee, who will then request opinions simultaneously from the two line judges. Any appeal made directly to line judges by a player or team or made after an excessive demonstration or complaint by the player(s) will be considered void and any appeal rights for that side for that particular rally will be forfeited.
1) **Kill Shot Appeals.** If the referee makes a call of "good" on a kill shot attempt which ends a rally, the loser of the rally may appeal the call. If the appeal is successful and the referee's original call reversed, the side which originally lost the rally is declared the winner of the rally. If the referee makes the call of "bad" or "skip" on a kill shot attempt, the rally has ended and the side against whom the call was made has the right to appeal the call if it felt the shot was good. If the appeal is successful and the referee's original call reversed, the referee must then decide if the shot could have been returned had play continued. If the shot could have been or was returned, the rally shall be replayed. If the shot was a kill or pass that the opponent could not have retrieved (in the referee's opinion), the side which originally lost the rally is declared the winner of the rally. The referee's judgment in this matter is final. When a rally is replayed, the server is entitled to two serves.
2) **Fault Serve Appeals.** If the referee makes a call of "fault" on a serve, the server may appeal the call. If the appeal is successful, the server is entitled to replay the serve. If the served ball was considered by the referee to be an ace, then a point shall be awarded to the server. If the referee makes "no call" on a serve (therefore indicating that the serve was "good"), either side may appeal. If the serve is overturned by the line judges, it will result in second serve or, if the appeal was made on the second serve, it will be loss of serve.
3) **Out Serve Appeals.** If the referee makes a call of "out serve" thereby stopping play, the serving side may appeal the call. If the appeal is successful, the referee shall revise the call to the proper call and the service shall be replayed, or a point awarded if the resulting serve was an ace. If the referee makes "no call", or calls a fault serve, and the receiver feels it was an out serve, the receiver may appeal. If the appeal is successful, the serve results in an out. Note: A safety zone violation by the server is an out serve.
4) **Double Bounce Pickup Appeals.** If the referee makes a call of "two bounces", thereby stopping play, the side against whom the call was made has the right of appeal. If the appeal is upheld, the rally is replayed or the referee may award the rally to the hitter if the resulting shot could not have been retrieved by the opponent

(and providing the referee's call did not cause the opponent to hesitate or stop play). If the referee makes "no call" on a particular play, indicating thereby that the player hit the ball before the second bounce, the opponent has the right to appeal at the end of the rally. However, since the ball is in play, the side wishing to appeal must clearly motion to the referee and linespeople by raising their non-racquet hand, thereby alerting the officials as to the exact shot which is being appealed. At the same time, the player appealing must continue to play. If the appealing player should lose the rally, and the appeal is upheld, the player who appealed then becomes the winner of the rally. All rallies replayed as the result of a double bounce pickup appeal shall result in the server getting two serves.

5) **Receiving Line (Encroachment) Violation Appeals.** If the referee makes a call of encroachment thereby stopping the play, the receiving side may appeal the call. If the appeal is successful, the service shall be replayed. If the referee makes no call and the server feels there was encroachment, the server may appeal. If the appeal is successful the service results in a point. (For safety zone violation by server or doubles partner, see 1.G.3.)

Rule 1. H. Rules Interpretations

If a player feels the referee has interpreted the rules incorrectly, the player may require the referee or Tournament Director to show him the applicable rule in the rulebook. Having discovered a misapplication or misinterpretation, the official must correct the error by replaying the rally, awarding the point, calling sideout, or taking whatever corrective measure necessary.

RULE 2. SERVE

Rule 2. A. Order

The player or team winning the coin toss has the option to serve or receive for the start of the first game. The second game will begin in reverse order of the first game. The player or team scoring the highest total of points in Games 1 and 2 will have the option to serve or receive for the start of the tiebreaker. In the event that both players or teams score an equal number of points in the first two games, another coin toss will take place and the winner of the toss will have the option to serve or receive.

Rule 2. B. Start

The serve is started from any place within the service zone. No part of either foot may extend beyond either line of the service zone. Stepping on, but not over the line, is permitted. The server must remain in the service zone from the moment the service motion begins until the served ball passes the short line. Violations are called "foot faults". The server may not start any service motion until the referee has called the score or second serve.

Rule 2. C. Manner

Once the service motion begins the ball is dropped or thrown to the floor while standing within the confines of the service zone and, on the first bounce is struck by the racquet so that the ball hits the front wall first and on rebound hits the floor behind the back edge of the short line, either with or without touching one of the side walls. A balk serve or fake swing at the ball is an infraction and is an out serve.

Rule 2. D. Readiness

Serves shall not be made until the referee has called the score or the second serve and the server has visually checked the receiver. The referee shall call the score as both server and receiver prepare to return to their respective position, shortly after the previous rally has ended.

Rule 2. E. Delays

Delays on the part of the server or receiver exceeding 10 seconds shall result in an out or point against the offender.

1) The 10-second rule is applicable to the server and receiver simultaneously. Collectively, they are allowed up to 10 seconds, after the score is called, to serve or be ready to receive. It is the server's responsibility to look and be certain the receiver is ready. If the receiver is not ready, he must signal so by raising his racquet above his head or completely turning his back to the server. (These are the only two acceptable signals.)

2) If the server serves the ball while the receiver is signaling "not ready", the serve shall go over with no penalty and the server shall be warned by the referee to check the receiver. If the server continues to serve without checking the receiver, the referee may award a technical for delay of game.

3) After the score is called, if the server looks at the receiver and the receiver is not signalling "not ready", the server may then serve. If the receiver attempts to signal "not ready" after that point, such signal shall not be acknowledged and the serve becomes legal.

RULE 3. SERVE IN DOUBLES

Rule 3. A. Server

At the beginning of each game in doubles, each side shall inform the referee of the order of service which shall be followed throughout the game. When the first server is out the first time up, the side is out. Thereafter, both players on each side shall serve until each receive a handout.

Rule 3. B. Partner's Position

On each serve, the server's partner shall stand erect with back to the sidewall and with both feet on the floor within the service box from the moment the server begins service motion until the served ball passes the short line. Violations are called "foot faults." However, if the server's partner enters the safety zone before the ball passes the short line the server loses service.

RULE 4. DEFECTIVE SERVES

Defective serves are of three types resulting in penalties as follows:

Rule 4. A. Dead-Ball Serve

A dead-ball serve results in no penalty and the server is given another serve (without cancelling a prior fault serve).

Rule 4. B. Fault Serve

Two fault serves result in a handout.

Rule 4. C. Out Serve

An out serve results in a handout.

RULE 5. DEAD-BALL SERVES

Dead-ball serves do not cancel any previous fault serve. The following are dead-ball serves:

Rule 5. A. Ball Hits Partner

A serve which strikes the server's partner while in the doubles box is a dead-ball serve. A serve which touches the floor before touching the server's partner is a short serve.

Rule 5. B. Screen Serve

A served ball which bases so closely to the server, or server's partner in the doubles box, as to obstruct the view of the returning side is a dead-ball serve.

Rule 5. C. Court Hinders

A serve that hits any part of the court, which under local rules is an obstruction, is a dead-ball serve.

Rule 5. D. Broken Ball

If the ball is determined to have broken on the serve, a new ball shall be substituted and the serve shall be replayed (not cancelling any prior fault serve).

RULE 6. FAULT SERVES

The following serves are faults and any two in succession result in an out:

Rule 6. A. Foot Faults

A foot fault results when:
1) The server does not begin the service motion with both feet in the service zone.
2) The server leaves the service zone before the ball passes the short line.
3) In doubles, the server's partner is not in the service box with both feet on the floor and back to the wall from the time the server begins the service motion until the ball passes the short line. (If the server, or doubles partner, enters into the safety zone before the served ball passes the short line, it shall result in the loss of serve.)

Rule 6. B. Short Service

A short serve is any served ball that first hits the front wall and on the rebound, hits the floor on or in front of the short line (with or without touching a side wall).

Rule 6. C. Three-Wall Serve

Any served ball that first hits the front wall and, on the rebound, strikes both side walls before touching the floor is a three-wall serve and a fault.

Rule 6. D. Ceiling Serve

Any served ball that first hits the front wall and, then touches the ceiling (with or without touching a side wall) is a fault.

Rule 6. E. Long Serve

A served ball that first hits the front wall and rebounds to the back wall before touching the floor (with or without touching a side wall) is a long serve and a fault.

Rule 6. F. Out-Of-Court Serve

Any served ball that first hits the front wall and, before striking the floor, goes out of the court.

RULE 7. OUT SERVES

Any of the following serves results in an out:

Rule 7. A. Two Consecutive Fault Serves

See Rule 6.

Rule 7. B. Failure to Serve Promptly

Failure of server to put the ball into play within 10 seconds of the calling of the score by the referee.

Rule 7. C Missed Serve Attempt

Any attempt to strike the ball that results in a total miss or in the ball touching any part of the server's body.

Rule 7. D. Non-Front Wall Serve

Any served ball that does not strike the front wall first.

Rule 7. E. Touched Serve

Any served ball that on the rebound from the front wall touches the server or server's racquet, or any ball intentionally stopped or caught by the server or server's partner.

Rule 7. F. Crotch Serve

If the served ball hits the crotch of the front wall and floor, front wall and sidewall, or front wall and ceiling it is an out serve (because it did not hit the front wall first). A serve into the crotch of the back wall and the floor is a good serve and in play. A served ball that hits the crotch of the side wall and floor beyond the short line is in play.

Rule 7. G. Illegal Hit

Any illegal hit (contacting the ball twice, carrying the ball, or hitting the ball with the handle of the racquet or part of the body or uniform) results in an out serve.

Rule 7. H. Fake or Balk Serve

Such a serve is defined as a non-continuous movement of the racquet towards the ball as the server drops the ball for the purpose of serving and results in an out serve.

Rule 7. I. Out-Of-Order Serve

In doubles, when either partner serves out-of-order the points scored by that server will be subtracted and an out serve will be called: if the second server serves out-of-order the out serve will be applied to the first server and the second server will resume serving. If the player designated as the first server serves out-of-order, a sideout will be called. In a match with line judges, the referee may enlist their aid to recall the number of points scored out-of-order.

Rule 7. J. Safety Zone Violation

If the server, or doubles partner, enters into the safety zone before the served ball passes the short line, it shall result in the loss of serve.

RULE 8. RETURN OF SERVE

Rule 8. A. Receiving Position

1) The receiver may not enter the safety zone until the ball bounces.
2) On the fly return attempt, the receiver may not strike the ball until the ball breaks the plane of the receiving (five-foot) line. The follow-through may carry the receiver or his racquet past the receiving line.
3) Neither the receiver nor his racquet may break the plane of the short line during the service return, except if the ball is struck after rebounding off the backwall. Any violation by the receiver results in a point for the server.

Rule 8. B. Defective Serve

A player on the receiving side may not intentionally catch or touch a served ball (such as an apparently long or short serve) until the referee has made a call or the ball has touched the floor for a second time. Violation results in a point.

Rule 8. C. Legal Return

After a legal serve, a player on the receiving team must strike the ball on the fly, or after the first bounce, and before the ball touches the floor the second time; and return the ball to the front wall, either directly or after touching one or both side walls, the back wall or the ceiling, or any combination of those surfaces. A returned ball may not touch the floor before touching the front wall (see 7.G.).

Rule 8. D. Failure To Return

The failure to return a serve results in a point for the server.

RULE 9. CHANGES OF SERVE

Rule 9. A. Outs

A server is entitled to continue serving until:
1) **Out serve.** See Rule 7.
2) **Two Consecutive Fault Serves.** See Rule 6.
3) **Ball Hits Partner.** Player hits partner with an attempted return.
4) **Failure to Return Ball.** Player or partner fails to hit the ball prior to its second bounce or fails to return the ball to the front wall on a fly, with or without hitting any combination of walls and ceiling.

5) **Avoidable Hinder.** Player or partner commits an avoidable hinder (Rule 12).

Rule 9. B. Sideout

In singles, a single handout or out equals a sideout and retires the server. In doubles, a single handout equals a sideout on the first service of each game; thereafter, two handouts equal a sideout which retires the serving team.

Rule 9. C. Effect of Sideout

When the server (or the serving team) receives a sideout, the server becomes the receiver and the receiver becomes the server.

RULE 10. RALLIES

Each legal return after the serve is called a rally. Play during rallies shall be according to the following rules:

Rule 10. A. Legal Hits

Only the head of the racquet may be used at any time to return the ball. The racquet may be held in one or both hands. Switching hands to hit a ball, touching the ball with any part of the body or uniform, or removing the wrist thong result in loss of the rally.

Rule 10. B. One Touch

In attempting returns, the ball may be touched or struck only once by a player or team or the result is a loss of rally. The ball may not be "carried." (A carried ball is one which rests on the racquet in such a way that the effect is more of a "sling" or "throw" than a hit.)

Rule 10. C. Failure To Return

Any of the following constitutes a failure to make a legal return during a rally:
1) the ball bounces on the floor more than once before being hit.
2) the ball does not reach the front wall on the fly.
3) the ball caroms off a player's racquet into a gallery or wall opening without first hitting the front wall.
4) a ball which obviously did not have the velocity or direction to hit the front wall strikes another player on the court.
5) a ball struck by one player on a team hits that or that player's partner.
6) committing an avoidable hinder (Rule 12).

Rule 10. D. Effect of Failure to Return

Violations of Rule 10 A., B. and C. result in a loss of rally. If the serving player or team loses the rally, it is an "out" (handout or sideout). If the receiver loses the rally, it results in a point for the server.

Rule 10. E. Return Attempts

1) In singles, if a player swings at, but misses the ball, the player may continue to attempt to return the ball until it touches the floor for the second time.

2) In doubles, if one player swings at, but misses the ball, both partners may make further attempts to return the ball until it touches the floor the second time. Both partners on a side are entitled to return the ball.

Rule 10. F. Out Of Court Ball

1) **After Return.** Any ball returned to the front wall which on the rebound or on the first bounce goes into the gallery or through any opening in a side wall shall be declared dead and the server shall receive two serves.

2) **No Return.** Any ball not returned to the front wall which caroms off a player's racquet into the gallery or into any opening in a sidewall either with or without touching the ceiling, side or back wall, shall be an out for the player failing to make the return, or a point for the opponent.

Rule 10. G. Broken Ball

If there is any suspicion that a ball has broken on the serve or during a rally, play shall continue until the end of the rally. The referee or any player may request the ball be examined. If the referee decides the ball is broken the ball will be replaced and the rally replayed. The server will get two serves. The only proper way to check for a broken ball is to squeeze it by hand. (Checking the ball by striking it with a racquet will not be considered a valid check and shall work to the disadvantage of the player or team which struck the ball after the rally.)

Rule 10. H. Play Stoppage

If a player loses a shoe or other equipment, or foreign objects enter the court, or any other outside interference occurs, the referee shall stop the play if such occurrence interferes with ensuing play or player's safety.

Rule 10. I. Replays

Whenever a rally is replayed for any reason, the server is awarded two serves. A previous fault serve is not considered.

RULE 11. DEAD-BALL HINDERS

A rally is replayed without penalty and the server receives two serves whenever a dead-ball hinder occurs.

Rule 11. A. SITUATIONS

1) **Court hinders.** Play stops when a ball hits any part of the court that was designated as a court hinder (such as a door handle); play also is stopped when the ball takes an irregular bounce off a rough or irregular surface which the referee determines affected the rally (such as a strange or dead bounce off a court light).

2) **Ball Hits Opponent.** When an opponent is hit by a return shot in flight, it is a dead-ball hinder. If the opponent is struck by a ball which obviously did not have the velocity or direction to reach the front wall, it is not a hinder, and

the player that hit the ball will lose the rally. A player who has been hit by the ball can stop play and make the call, though the call must be made immediately and acknowledged by the referee.

3) **Body Contact.** If body contact occurs which the referee believes was sufficient to stop the rally, either for the purpose of preventing injury by further contact or because the contact prevented a player from being able to make a reasonable return, the referee shall award a hinder. Body contact, particularly on the follow-through, is not necessarily a hinder.

4) **Screen ball.** Any ball rebounding from the front wall close to the body of a player on the side which just hit the ball and which interferes with, or prevents, the returning player or side from seeing the ball.

5) **Back Swing Hinder.** Any body contact, either on the backswing or en route to or just prior to returning the ball, which impairs the hitter's ability to take a reasonable swing. This call may be made by the player attempting the return if it is made immediately. This call can be made by the player attempting the return, though the call must be made immediately and is subject to the approval of the referee. Note: the interference may be construed as an avoidable hinder (See Rule 12. E.).

6) **Safety Holdup.** Any player about to execute a return who believes he is likely to strike his opponent with the ball or racquet may immediately stop play and request a dead ball hinder. This call must be made immediately and is subject to acceptance and approval of the referee. (The referee wil grant a dead-ball hinder if he believes the holdup was reasonable and the player would have been able to return the shot, and the referee may also call an avoidable hinder if warranted.)

7) **Other Interference.** Any other intentional interference which prevents an opponent from having a fair chance to see or return the ball. Example: The ball obviously skids after striking a wet spot on the court floor or wall.

Rule 11 B. Effect of Hinders

The referee's call of hinder stops play and voids any situation which follows, such as the ball hitting the player. The only hinders a player may call are specified in 11. A. 2, 11. A. 5 andn 11. A. 6, and are subject to the approval of the referee. A dead-ball hinder stops play and the rally is replayed. The server receives two serves.

Rule 11. C. Avoidance

While making an attempt to return the ball, a player is entitled to a fair chance to see and return the ball. It is the responsibility of the side that has just hit the ball to move so the receiving side may go straight to the ball and have an unobstructed view of the ball after it leaves the front wall. In the judgment of the referee however, the receiver must make a reasonable effort to move towards the ball and have a reasonable chance to return the ball in order for a hinder to be called.

Rule 12. AVOIDABLE HINDERS (Point or Sideout Hinder)

An avoidable hinder results in the loss of a rally. An avoidable hinder does not necessarily have to be an "intentional" act and is a result of any of the following:

Rule 12. A. Failure To Move

Does not move sufficiently to allow an opponent a shot.

Rule 12. B. Blocking

Moves into a position which blocks the opponent from getting to, or returning, the ball; or in doubles, a player moves in front of an opponent as the player's partner is returning the ball.

Rule 12. C. Moving Into The Ball

Moves in the way and is struck by the ball just played by the opponent.

Rule 12. D. Pushing

Deliberately pushes or shoves opponent during a rally.

Rule 12. E. Restricts Opponent's Swing

Moves, or fails to move, so that the player returning the ball does not have a free, unimpeded swing.

Rule 12. F. Intentional Distractions

Deliberate shouting, stamping of feet, waving of racquet, or any manner of disrupting the player who is hitting the ball.

Rule 12. G. Wetting The Ball

The players, particularly the server, have the responsibility that the ball is kept dry at all times. Any wetting of the ball either deliberate or by accident, that is not corrected prior to the beginning of the rally, shall result in an avoidable hinder.

RULE 13. TIMEOUTS

Rule 13. A. Rest Periods

Each player or team is entitled to three 30-second timeouts in games to 15 and two 30-second timeouts in games to 11. Timeouts may not be called by either side after service motion has begun. Calling for a timeout when none remain or after service motion has begun, or taking more than 30 seconds in a timeout, will result in the assessment of a technical for delay of game.

Rule 13. B. Injury

If a player is injured during the course of a match as a result of contact with the ball, racquet, opponent, wall or floor, he shall be granted an injury timeout. An injured player shall not be allowed more than a total of 15 minutes of rest during the match. If thee injured player is not able to resume play after total rest of 15 minutes, the match shall be awarded

to the opponent. Muscle cramps and pulls, fatigue, and other ailments that are not caused by direct contact on the court will not be considered an injury.

Rule 13. C. Equiment Timeouts

Players are expected to keep all clothing and equipment in good, playable condition and are expected to use regular timeouts and time betweenn games for adjustment and replacement of equipment. If a player or team is out of timeouts and the referee determines that an equipment change or adjustment is necessary for fair and safe continuation of the match, the referee may award an equipment timeout not to exceed two minutes.

Rule 13. D. Between Games

The rest period between the first two games of a match is two minutes. If a tiebreaker is necessary, the rest period between the second and third game is five minutes.

Rule 13. E. Postponed Games

Any games postponed by referees shall be resumed with the same score as when postponed.

RULE 14. TECHNICALS

Rule 14. A. Technical Fouls

The referee is empowered to deduct one point from a player's or team's score when in the referee's sole judgment, the player is being overtly and deliberately abusive. The actual invoking of this penalty is called a "Referee's Technical". If after the technical is called against the abusing player, and the play is not immediately continued, the referee is empowered to forfeit the match in favor of the abusing player's opponent. Some examples of actions which may result in technicals are:

1) Profanity. Profanity is an automatic technical and should be invoked by the referee whenever it occurs.
2) Excessive arguing.
3) Threat of any nature to opponent or referee.
4) Excessive or hard striking of the ball between rallies.
5) Slamming of the racquet against walls or floor, slamming the door, or any action which might result in injury to the court or other players.
6) Delay of game, either in the form of taking too much time during time-outs and between games, in drying the court, in excessive questioning of the referee on the rules, or in excessive or unnecessary appeals.
7) Intentional front line foot faults to negate a bad lob serve.
8) Anything considered to be unsportsmanlike behavior.
9) Player under age of 19 who fails to wear eyeguards or wear them properly. (See E. 2. UNIFORM in Section 2 on Page 7.)

Rule 14. B. Technical Warning

If a player's behavior is not so severe as to warrant a referee's technical, a technical warning may be issued without point deduction.

Rule 14. C. Effect of Technical or Warning

If a referee issues a technical warning, it shall not result in a loss of rally or point and shall be accompanied by a brief explanation of the reason for the warning. If a referee issues a referee's technical, one point shall be removed from the offender's score. The awarding of the technical shall have no effect on serve changes or sideouts. If the technical occurs either between games or when the offender has no points, the result will be that the offender's score will revert to a minus one (-1).

RULE 15. PROFESSIONAL

A professional is defined as any player (male, female, or junior) who accepts prize money regardless of the amount in any PRO SANCTIONED tournaments including WPRA, RMA, and other events so deemed by the AARA Board of Directors.

1) A player may participate in a PRO SANCTIONED tournament which awards cash prizes, but will not be considered a professional if no prize money is accepted.
2) The acceptance by a player of merchandise or travel expenses shall not be considered as prize money, and thus does not jeopardize a player's amateur status.

RULE 16. RETURN TO AMATEUR STATUS

Any player who has been classified as a professional (see Rule 15) can recover amateur status by requesting, in writing, this desire to be reclassified as an amateur. This application shall be tendered to the Executive Director of the American Amateur Racquetball Association (AARA), or his designated representative, and shall become effective immediately as long as the player making application for reinstatement of amateur status has received no money in any pro sanctioned tuornament, as defined in Rule 15, for the past 12 months.

RULE 17. AGE GROUP DIVISIONS

Age is determined as of the first day of the tournament:

MEN'S AGE DIVISIONS:
Open—All players other than Pro
Junior Veterans—19+
Junior Veterans—25+
Veterans—30+
Seniors—35+
Veteran Seniors—40+
Masters—45+
Veteran Masters—50+
Golden Masters—55+
Senior Golden Masters—60+
Veteran Golden Masters—65+
Advanced Golden Masters—70+

OTHER DIVISIONS:
Mixed Doubles
Disabled

JUNIOR DIVISIONS:
Age determined as of January 1st of each calendar year.

JUNIOR BOYS' AND GIRLS' AGE DIVISIONS:
18 & under
16 & under
14 & under
12 & under
10 & under
8 & under (no-bounce)
Doubles Team—ages apply as above

Rule 17. A. Junior Division Exceptions
Junior Players should abide by all AARA rules with the following exceptions:

1) **Scoring.** All matches in Junior divisions will be the best of two games to 15 points, win by 1 point. If a tiebreaker (third game) is necessary, the game is played to 11 points.
2) **Eye Protection.** Eye protection must be worn in all AARA junior sanctioned events. (See Sec. 2. E. UNIFORM 2 for penalty for violation.)
3) **Timeouts.** Three in each game.

4—TOURNAMENTS

RULE 18. DRAWS

a) If possible, all draws shall be made at least two days before the tournament commences. The seeding method of drawing shall be approved by the American Amateur Racquetball Association (AARA).
b) The draw and seeding committee shall be chaired by the AARA's Executive Director, National Commissioner, and the host Tournament Director. No other persons shall participate in the draw or seeding unless at the invitation of the draw and seeding committee.
c) In local, state and regional tournaments the draw shall be the responsiblity of the tournament chairperson. In regional play the tournament chairperson should work in coordination with the AARA Regional Commissioner at the tournament.

RULE 19. SCHEDULING

Rule 19. A. Preliminary Matches
If one or more contestants are entered in both singles and doubles, they may be required to play both singles and doubles on the same day or night with little rest between matches. This is a risk assumed on entering both singles and doubles events. If possible, the schedule should provide at least a one hour rest period between matches.

Rule 19. A. Final Matches
Where one or more players have reached the finals in both singles and doubles, it is recommended that the doubles match be played on the day preceding the singles. This would assure more rest between the

final matches. If both final matches must be played on the same day or night, the following procedure is recommended.

1. The singles match be played first.
2. A rest period of not less than one hour be allowed between the finals in singles and doubles.

Rule 20. NOTICE OF MATCHES

After the first round of matches, it is the responsibility of each player to check the posted schedules to determine the time and place of each subsequent match. If any change is made in the schedule after posting, it shall be the duty of the committee or tournament director to notify the players of the change.

Rule 21. THIRD PLACE

Players are not required to play off for 3rd place or 4th place. However, for point standings, if one semifinalist wants to play off for third and the semifinalist does not, the one willing to play shall be awarded third place. If both semifinalists do not wish to play off for 3rd and 4th positions, then the points shall be awarded evenly.

Rule 22. AARA REGIONAL TOURNAMENTS

AARA Regional Tournaments—The United States and Europe are divided into a combined total of 16 regions.

a) A player may compete in only one regional tournament per year.
b) The defined area of eligibility for a person's region is that of their permanent residence. The players are encouraged to participate in their own region; However, for the purpose of convenience they may participate outside their region.
c) A player can participate in only two events in a regional tournament.
d) Awards and remuneration to the AARA National Championships will be posted on the entry blank.

Rule 23. TOURNAMENT MANAGEMENT

In all AARA sanctioned tournaments, the tournament director and/or the National AARA official in attendance may decide on a change of court after the completion of any tournament game if such a change will accommodate better spectator conditions.

Rule 24. TOURNAMENT CONDUCT

In all AARA sanctioned tournaments, the referee is empowered to default a match if the conduct of a player or team is considered detrimental to the tournament and the game. (See Rule 1. E. 5).

RULE 25. AARA ELIGIBILITY

Any paid-up AARA member in good standing, who has not been classified as a professional (See Rule 15) may compete in any AARA sanctioned tournament.

RULE 26. AARA NATIONAL CHAMPIONSHIP

The National Singles, Junior and National Doubles are separate tournaments and are played on different weekends. There will be a consolation round in all divisions.

Rule 26. A. Regional Qualifications

1) The National Ratings Committee may handle the rating of each region and determine how many players shall qualify from each regional tournament.
2) All national finalists in each division may be exempt from qualifying for the same division the following year.
3) There may be a tournament one day ahead of the National Tournament at the same site to qualify 8 players in each division who were unable to qualify or who failed to qualify in the Regionals.
4) This rule is in force only when a region is obviously over subscribed.

Rule 26. B. Definition of Regions

1) **Qualifying Singles.** A player may have to qualify at one of the 16 regional tournaments.
2) **Qualifying Doubles.** There will be no regional qualifying for doubles.

AARA REGIONS

Region 1—Maine, New Hampshire, Vermont, Massachusetts, Rhode Island, Connecticut
Region 2—New York, New Jersey
Region 3—Pennsylvania, Maryland, Virginia, Delaware, District of Columbia
Region 4—Florida, Georgia, North Carolina, South Carolina
Region 5—Alabama, Mississippi, Tennessee
Region 6—Arkansas, Kansas, Missouri, Oklahoma
Region 7—Texas, Louisiana
Region 8—Wisconsin, Iowa, Illinois
Region 9—West Virginia, Ohio, Michigan
Region 10—Indiana, Kentucky
Region 11—North Dakota, South Dakota, Minnesota, Nebraska
Region 12—Arizona, New Mexico, Utah, Colorado
Region 13—Wyoming, Montana
Region 14—Nevada, California, Hawaii
Region 15—Washington, Idaho, Oregon, Alaska
Region 16—Americans in Europe

RULE 27. NATIONAL JUNIOR CHAMPIONSHIP

It will be conducted on a separate date and location under the same parameters as Rule 26 A. & B.

RULE 28. INTERCOLLEGIATE TOURNAMENT

It will be conducted at a separate date and location.

5—ONE-WALL AND THREE-WALL RULES

RULE 29. ONE-WALL AND THREE-WALL RULES

Basically racquetball rules for one-wall, three-wall and four-wall are the same with the following exception:

One-Wall: Court Size—wall shall be 20 ft. in width and 16 ft. high, floor 20 ft. in width and 34 ft. from the wall to the back edge of the long line. There should be a minimum of three feet beyond the long line and six feet outside each side line and behind the long line to permit movement area for the players.

Short Line—Back edge sixteen (16) feet from the wall.

Service Markers—Lines at least 6 inches long parallel to and midway between the long and short lines, extending in from the side lines. The imaginary extension and joining of these lines indicates the service line. Lines are 1½ inches in width.

Service Zone—Floor area inside and including the short, side and service lines.

Receiving Zone—Floor area in back of short line bounded by and including the long and side lines.

Three-Wall Serve—A serve that goes beyond the side walls on the fly, is considered "long." A serve that goes beyond the long line on a fly, but within the side walls is the same as "short."

Court Size—short side wall—20′ in width and 20′ in length. Side wall shall extend back on either side from the front wall parallel 20′ along the side wall markers. Side wall may extend from 20′ at the front wall and taper down to 12′ at the end of the side wall. All other markings are the same as 4-wall.

Court Size—long side wall—20′ in width and 20′ in height and 40′ in length. Side walls shall extend back on either side 40′. The side wall may, but is not restricted to, tapering from 20′ of height at the front wall down to 12 feet at the 40′ marker. All lines are the same as in 4-wall racquetball.

6—RULES FOR 8 & UNDER FREE BOUNCE

RULE 30. USE AARA RACQUETBALL RULES WITH THESE MODIFCATIONS:

After a legal serve, the ball may bounce as many times as the receiver wants until the player swings once to return the ball to the front wall. (In other words, they get one swing at the ball to get it back.)

The ball may be hit after the serve or during a rally at any time, but *must* be hit *before* it crosses the *short line* on its way *back* to the front wall.

The receiver can hit the ball before it hits the back wall or may play it off the back wall but cannot cross the short line *after* the ball contacts the back wall.

The only exception to crossing the short line is if the ball is returned to the back wall from the front wall on the fly (without touching the floor) then the receiver may cross the short line and play the ball on the first bounce.

New additions are lines on the front wall (use tape) at 3-feet and 1-foot high. If the ball is hit below the 3-foot and above the 1-foot line during a rally, it has to be returned before it bounces the third time. If the ball hits below the 1-foot line during a rally, it must be played or returned to the front wall before it bounces twice as in regulation racquetball. This gives incentive to keep the ball low.

Matches are best 2 out of 3 games to 11 points.

7—NATIONAL WHEELCHAIR RACQUETBALL ASSOCIATION OFFICIAL RULES OF WHEELCHAIR RACQUETBALL

For rules, contact AARA.

8—HOW TO REFEREE WHEN THERE IS NO REFEREE

Rule 1—SAFETY

SAFETY IS THE PRIMARY AND OVER-RIDING RESPONSIBILITY OF EVERY PLAYER WHO ENTERS THE COURT. At *no time* should the physical safety of the participants be compromised. Players are entitled, AND EXPECTED, to hold up their swing, WITHOUT PENALTY, any time they believe there might be a risk of physical contact. Any time a player says he held up to avoid contact, even if he was over-cautious, he is entitled to a hinder (rally replayed without penalty).

Rule 2—SCORE

Since there is no referee, or scorekeeper, it is important to see that there is no misunderstanding in this area, so THE SERVER IS REQUIRED to announce both the server's and receiver's score before EVERY first serve.

Rule 3—DURING RALLIES

During rallies, it is generally the *hitter's* responsiblity to make the call—if there is a possibility of a skip ball, double-bounce, or illegal hit, play should continue until the *hitter* makes the call against himself. If the hitter does not make the call against himself and goes on to win the rally, and the player thought that one of the hitter's shots was not good, he may "appeal" to the hitter by pointing out which shot he though was bad and request the hitter to reconsider. If the hitter is sure of his call, AND the opponent is still sure the hitter is wrong, the rally is replayed. As a matter of etiquette, players are expected to make calls against themselves any time they are not sure. In other words, if a shot is very close as to whether or not it was a good kill or a skip ball, unless the hitter is *sure* the shot was good, he should call it a skip.

Rule 4—SERVICE

a) **Fault Serves (Long, Short, Ceiling & Three-Wall).** The Receiver has the primary responsibility to make these calls, and again, he should give the benefit of the doubt to his opponent whenever it is close. The receiver must make his call immediately, and not wait until he hits the ball and has the benefit of seeing how good a shot he can hit. It is not an option play...the receiver does not have the right to play a short serve just because he thinks it's a setup.

b) **Screen Serves.** When there is no referee, a screen serve does not become an option play. When the receiver believes his vision of the ball was sufficiently impaired as to give the server too great an advantage on the serve, the receiver may hold up his swing and call a screen serve, or, if he still feels he can make a good shot at the ball, he can say nothing and continue playing. He may not call a screen after he attempts to hit the ball. Further, the server may not call a screen under any circumstances...he must simply expect to have to play the rally until he hears a call from the receiver. (In doubles, unless the ball goes behind the back of the server's partner, no screens should be called.)

c) **Others.** Foot faults, 10 second violations, receiving-line violations, service-zone infringement and other "technical" calls really require a referee. However, if either player believes his opponent is abusing any of these rules, between rallies, he should discuss it with his opponent to be sure there is agreement on what the rule is, and to put each other on notice that the rules should be followed.

Rule 5—HINDERS

Generally, the hinder should work like the screen serve—as an option play for the hindered party. *Only* the person going for the shot can stop play by calling a hinder, and he must do so immediately—not wait until he has the benefit of seeing how good a shot he can hit. If the hindered party believes he can make an effective return in spite of some physical contact or screen that has occurred, he may continue to play.

Rule 6—AVOIDABLE HINDERS

Since avoidable hinders are usually not intentional, they do occur even in the friendliest matches. The player who realizes he made such an error should simply award the rally to his opponent. If a player feels his opponent was guilty of an avoidable, and the player did not call it on himself, the "offended" player should appeal to his opponent by pointing out that he thought it was an avoidable. The player may then call it on himself, or disagree, but the call can only be made on yourself. Often, just pointing out what you think is an avoidable will put the player on notice for future rallies and prevent recurrence.

Rule 7—DISPUTES

If either player, for any reason, desires to have a referee, it is considered common courtesy for the other player to go along with the request and a referee suitable to both sides should be found. If there is not a referee, and a question about a rule or rule interpretation comes up, seek out the club pro or a more experienced player. Then, after the match, contact your local state racquetball association for the answer.

GLOSSARY

ACE: A winning legal serve that completely eludes a receiver.

ANTICIPATION: The skill of learning the angles of the ball as it travels around the court and moving to the correct position in time to return it.

APEX: When the ball reaches its highest point after it bounces from the floor.

AROUND-THE-WALL BALL: A shot that strikes three walls. It must hit the side wall first, then the front wall and finally the opposite side wall.

AVOIDABLE HINDER: A player's intentional interference of an opponent's shot.

"B" PLAYER: A player whose tournament skill level is average.

BACK COURT: The area of the court which extends ten feet from the back wall.

BACKHAND: The stroke used to hit the ball starting from the side of the body opposite the hitting hand.

BACKHAND GRIP: The manner in which the racquet is held for shots to the backhand. Usually a ¼ inch counterclockwise rotation from the forehand grip.

BACK-INTO-BACK WALL SHOT: A ball that is driven into the rear wall and travels on the fly to the front wall.

BACK SWING: The act in which the racquet is brought back behind the body from the ready position to prepare for the forward swing.

BACK WALL: The rear wall.

BACK WALL SHOT: Striking the ball towards the front wall after it rebounds from the rear wall.

BLOCK: Moving your body in front of your opponent, thus preventing him from seeing the ball.

BODY CONTACT: Contact with your opponent during play which the referee believes sufficient to stop the rally. A hinder is then called.

BUMPER GUARD: The protective covering on the outer rim of a racquet.

BYE: A pass from the first round of a tournament to the second round without having to play a match.

CEILING SERVE: A serve that strikes the ceiling after hitting the front wall resulting in a fault or bad serve.

CEILING SHOT: A ball that strikes the ceiling, then rebounds to the floor and bounces deep into the court (sometimes called the CEILING BALL).

CENTER COURT: Roughly the area of the court between the receiving line and the service line.

CENTER COURT CONTROL: Maintaining center court position during a game while forcing your opponent to return the ball from deep in the court.

CENTER COURT POSITION: Considered to be the most strategic position in the court, it is located in the center of the court about two to four feet behind the short line.

CHANGE-OF-PACE SHOT: A shot that changes the tempo of play.

CONSOLATION: A bracket in a tournament that permits entrants who lose in the first round an opportunity to continue play against other first round losers.

CONTROL: The ability to hit the ball to an intended spot on the court.

COURT: The playing area of the court with dimensions of 40' long by 20' wide by 20' in height.

COURT HINDERS: An interference of the ball during play by an obstruction in the court other than the normal playing area.

CRACK BALL: A ball that strikes the side wall and floor making a return virtually impossible.

CROSSCOURT PASS SHOT: A pass that strikes the front wall, then rebounds against the side wall, opposite your opponent (a wide-angle pass shot).

CROTCH: A juncture of two playing surfaces in the court.

CROWDING: Playing too close to your opponent.

CUTTHROAT: A racquetball game played by three players.

DEAD BALL: A ball that is no longer in play.

DEFAULT: Any player that is either unable to play or declines to play, thereby losing the game.

DEFECTIVE SERVE: When the receiver intentionally catches or touches a served ball (such as a long or short serve) before it is called by the referee or hits the floor twice.

DEFENSIVE SHOT: Any shot that is executed in such a way so as to continue the rally.

DIE: A ball that loses momentum or slows down after striking a wall.

DIG: To retrieve a very low shot before it hits the floor a second time.

DONUT: Zero points scored in a game.

DOUBLES: A game where two teams with two players each compete.

DOWN-THE-LINE SHOT: A pass or kill shot that follows parallel to a side wall.

DRAW: The selection of participants to determine the order of play in a tournament.

DRIVE SERVE: See Power Serve.

DRIVE SHOT: A shot hit very hard which only strikes the front wall, then the floor.

DROP SHOT: A delicate shot hit with little speed, usually from front court.

ERROR: Failing to return a ball during play.

EYEGUARDS: Safety glasses or safety guards worn to protect the player's eyes from injury by the ball and racquet.

FAULT: A ball that is served illegally.

FLAT ROLLOUT: A kill shot that strikes the front wall low enough so that it rebounds without a bounce.

FLOAT: A ball traveling so slowly that your opponent has time to get to it and setup for a very easy shot.

FLY SHOT: Hitting a ball after it rebounds from the front wall and before it hits the floor.

FOLLOW-THROUGH: The completion of the stroke after hitting the ball with the racquet.

FOOT FAULT: A serve that is declared illegal because the server or his doubles partner violated the rule pertaining to the location of the feet while serving.

FOOTWORK: Moving your feet in relation to the rest of your body during play.

FOREHAND: A stroke hit across your body from the same side as the hand with which you play.

FRONT COURT: The area of the court between the front wall and the service line.

FRONT AND BACK FORMATION: A doubles formation in which one partner controls the front half of the court and the other partner controls the back half.

FRONT WALL-SIDE WALL KILL SHOT: A kill shot that strikes the front wall first and then the side wall.

GAME: The scoring of twenty-one points.

GAME POINT: The point that will make the player or team the winner of the game.

GARBAGE SERVE: A low lob serve that hits the front wall and lands about four feet behind the short line and then bounces in a medium arc forcing the receiver to return the serve from shoulder height.

GARFINKEL SERVE: A crosscourt or Z serve to the opponent's forehand.

HALF-VOLLEY: Hitting a ball immediately after it strikes the floor.

HANDOUT: Loss of service of the first server of a doubles team.

HEAD OF RACQUET: The hitting surface of the racquet.

HINDER: An unintentional interference of an opponent during play.

I-FORMATION: A means of dividing court responsibilities between two players of a doubles team with one player covering the front and his partner the back.

KILL SHOT: Hitting low on the front wall with a ball that is either impossible or nearly impossible to return.

LIVE BALL: A ball that is legally in play.

LOB SERVE: A ball that is hit high and softly on the front wall that rebounds to the deep court in a high angling arc near a side wall.

LOB SHOT: A shot that is hit high and softly and strikes the front wall high enough so it will rebound high towards the back wall.

LONG SERVE: A serve that strikes the back wall without first bouncing or striking the floor.

MASTERS DIVISION: The division of play in which a participant must be at least 45 years of age.

MATCH: The winner of two games out of three.

MATCH POINT: The point that will make the player or team the winner of the match.

MID-COURT: The area of the court roughly defined as between the serving line and the receiving line.

MIXED DOUBLES: Doubles play in which a male and female team up and play against another male and female.

NON-FRONT WALL SERVE: A serve that hits the floor, side wall or ceiling before it strikes the front wall.

NOVICE: A beginner or unskilled player.

OFFENSIVE SHOT: A shot that is designed to end a rally (e.g., kill shot).

OUT: An illegal serve that results in a loss of serve, normally called a SIDEOUT.

OUT-OF-ORDER SERVE: In doubles play, when one of the partners does not serve in the designated order.

OUT SERVE: Results in the serve going to the opponent.

OVERHEAD SHOT: Hitting a ball above your head.

PASS SHOT: Hitting a ball out of your opponent's reach.

PHOTON: An extremely hard hit shot.

PINCH SHOT: A shot that hits the side wall, then the front wall and then rebounds toward the opposite side wall.

PLACE SHOT: To hit the ball accurately to a particular area of the front wall or the court.

PLUM: An easy setup.

POINT: A unit of scoring.

POINT OF CONTACT: The point where the racquet meets the ball.

POWER SERVE: A serve that is hit so that it rebounds fast and low from the front wall to a rear corner of the court.

PUMPKIN: An easy setup.

RALLY: A series of hits between players from the serve until the point is over.

READY POSITION: The stance the receiver takes while waiting for the serve.

RECEIVER: The player who is waiting to receive the serve.

RECEIVING LINE: The line that is five feet behind the short line.

REFEREE: The individual who makes all the calls during a match.

REKILL: When a player hits an opponent's kill attempt for a kill shot of his own.

REST PERIOD: There are three 30 second time-outs in games to 15 and two 30 second time-outs in games to 11 points. A player receives a two minute rest between the first two games and a five minute rest between the second and third games.

ROLLOUT: A ball that strikes the front wall so low that it does not bounce on the rebound but instead, "rolls out" on the floor.

SAFETY ZONE: The five foot area bounded by the short line and the receiving line.

SCREEN BALL: Any ball that passes too close to a player, obstructing his opponent's view and ability to return the ball.

SCREEN SERVE: A served ball which passes so closely to the server or server's partner as to obstruct the view for the returning side.

SENIORS DIVISION: This is the division of competition in which a participant must be at least 35 years of age.

SERVE: Method of putting the ball into play.

SERVER: Person who puts the ball into play.

SERVICE BOX: The area at both ends of the service zone where the non-serving doubles partner must stand until the ball passes the short line.

SERVICE LINE: The line that is five feet in front of and parallel to the short line and fifteen feet from the front wall.

SERVICE ZONE: The five foot area between the outer edges of the service line and the short line.

SET POSITION: The ready position in preparation for the stroke.

SETUP: A ball that can be easily returned for a kill shot.

SHOOT: An attempt to hit a kill shot.

SHOOTER: A player who depends heavily on the kill shot.

SHORT LINE: The line that is located in the middle of the court five feet behind the service line.

SHORT SERVE: A served ball that rebounds from the front wall and bounces in front of or on the short line. Two of these serves in succession results in a loss of serve.

SIDE BY SIDE: Means of dividing court responsibilities between two players of a doubles team with one player generally covering balls on the right, with his partner covering the balls on the left.

SIDEOUT: Loss of service.

SIDE WALL-FRONT WALL KILL SHOT: A kill shot in which the ball strikes the side wall first, then the front wall (commonly called the pinch shot).

SINGLES: A game in which one player plays against another player.

SKIP BALL: A ball that strikes the floor before hitting the front wall.

STRAIGHT KILL: A ball that rebounds from the front wall on the same path.

TECHNICAL: A judgment call by the referee during tournament play due to unsportsmanlike conduct.

THONG: The nylon strap that is attached to the butt of the racquet and wrapped around the wrist of the player.

TOUCH: Superb racquet control.

THREE-WALL SERVE: An illegal serve that connects with three walls on the fly.

TOUR OF THE COURT: A rally where one player exerts little effort in controlling the play and runs his opponent all over the court.

UNAVOIDABLE HINDER: Unintentional actions which result in an inability to return the ball (i.e. ball hits opponent, screen ball, safety holdup, etc.)

VOLLEY: Hitting a ball in the air before it strikes the ground (commonly called a fly shot).

WALLPAPER BALL: A ball that hugs the side wall as it travels to the rear area of the court, making it difficult for a return.

WINNERS: Shots that end a rally.

WRIST SNAP: Breaking or snapping of the wrist which adds power to a stroke. It must occur at the point of impact with the ball.

Z BALL: A shot that strikes the front wall first, the side wall, and then the opposite side wall in the rear of the court.

Z SERVE: A serve in which the ball strikes the front wall, the side wall, then bounces behind the short line and hits the opposite side wall in the rear of the court.

— NOTES —

INDEX

— NOTES —

— NOTES —

— NOTES —

— NOTES —